Joe Sixpack
PMB 120
8500 Henry Ave.
Philadelphia, Pa., 19128

Printed in the United States of America.

First Edition: September 2011
ISBN-13: 978-1463789817
ISBN-10: 1463789815

What the
Hell
am I
Drinking?

Joe Sixpack

The German

The British Isles

The Belgians

The Americans

To every brewer
who ever made me a beer.

I thank you from the bottom of my glass.

Forward

If you've ever attended the annual Great American Beer Festival in Denver, you have a good idea of the huge variety of beer styles on the shelves today. The event is the world's largest judged beer competition, with gold, silver and bronze medals awarded in more than 80 different style categories, from Düsseldorf-style altbier to American-style wheat-wine ale.

Please don't ask me to name 'em all. And forget about the 80-plus subcategories: I'm fairly certain I couldn't detect the difference between, say, a Kristalweizen and a Leichtes weizen, even if you held a Luger to my head.

Too many? Too few? Either way, the credit for this lovely mess o' beer goes to Michael Jackson, the late, great British newspaperman and beer critic.

He's the one who invented the notion of definable beer styles in 1977, with the publication of his groundbreaking "The World Guide to Beer."

Before his book, we didn't much reckon with the methods, ingredients, flavors and cultural traditions behind the various types of beer around the globe. We tended to call it "British beer" or "German beer" or whatever, even if the beer within each country varied greatly from one town to the next. Beer drinkers surely could taste the difference between a bitter and a mild. But outside of technical brewing manuals, there was no clear understanding of what made them different and why.

"Michael's book really opened a lot of people's minds and introduced people to the concept that there were all these kinds of beers that were brewed around the world," said Charlie Papazian, president of the Brewers Association which runs the festival. "He was the one who showed that these beers had tradition and different qualities attributed to ingredients and aging and fermentation and other unique characteristics."

In an age when the association recognizes no fewer than five different types of Belgian-style sour ale alone, it's almost quaint to look back at the 30-year-old book. Jackson's guide laid out just 24 "classical beer styles," roughly grouping them as ales, lagers and wheat beer.

For those of us who suffered a generation ago with little other than boring American industrial lager, it read like an  anthropology journal, with Jackson lovingly describing the history, flavor and people behind these unheard-of styles. Rauchbier from Bamberg, white beer from Leuven, pale ale from Burton—Jackson explained why each was worthy of appreciation.

American beer lovers, looking for something different, drooled. Some took action.

In Seattle, Charles Finkel of the Merchant du Vin wine importing company, gave up the grapes and used the book to track down exotic beers around the world. Suddenly classic but little-seen labels like Samuel Smith's and Lindemans were showing up on American shelves.

Homebrewers began to replicate the styles—Russian stout, Berliner weisse, Scotch ales, beers that had never been tasted outside of their homelands.

The style descriptions evolved. Where Jackson had simply mentioned their general specifications, others established technical guidelines, including original gravity, alcohol content, bittering units, color definitions and other elements. By 1989, beer historian Fred Eckhardt's "The Essentials of Beer Style" identified specific brewing details for 38 styles worldwide.

The list continued to grow.

Papazian, a home-brewing pioneer, personally paged through every issue of the German brewing magazine *Brauindustrie*, gleaning the specs originally authored by brewing professor Anton Piendl. *Zymurgy*, the journal of the American Homebrewers Association, published the standards for innovative do-it-yourselfers.

U.S. craft brewers began creating their own knockoffs, with distinct American interpretations of pale ale, stout, barleywine and even wheat beer. Suddenly, a brown ale was no longer just a brown ale. It might be an English version, like mild Newcastle; or Flemish, like sweet and sour Goudenband; or American, like hoppy Pete's Wicked.

Other styles seemingly evolved from nowhere.

In the mid-1990s, dozens of brewers started making raspberry wheat beer. It was as if there was no other fruit on the planet. So in 1998, the GABF added a raspberry beer category.

It disappeared three years later.

A few years ago, the festival added coffee-flavored beer. Then pumpkin. Other newbies include gluten-free, low-strength, American-style sour, American-style imperial stout and... well you catch my drift. The GABF has ensured that the list will continue to morph with new hybrids, thanks to its medal for the "best experimental beer."

I argued once that, perhaps, the festival has gone overboard with awarding medals in all these styles. Wouldn't beer drinkers be better served if the festival named a single best of show? America demands one big winner. We play the World Series and crown one champion, not six division winners. We've got one best picture at the Academy Awards. One Best in Show at the Westminster Kennel Club. One Miss America.

But after Michael's death in 2007, I reconsidered. Every one of those medals—and each one of the styles in this guide—is a tribute to the guy who convinced us why we should care about beer.

So, that's why I wrote this book.

A simple glass of beer is not so simple any more. In my home state of Pennsylvania, for example, there are now more than 4,000 different brands for sale. Some are classic, old styles that are finally winning new recognition. Others are wholly new inventions, the product of incredibly imaginative and talented brewers. We are quite simply living in the absolute best time in the entire history of mankind to drink beer. Yet, all of this great and wondrous beer leaves me with one important question:

What the hell am I drinking?

The classical beer-styles
(circa 1977)

"Beers fall into three broad categories," Michael Jackson wrote in *The World Guide to Beer*: top-fermented, bottom-fermented and wheat beer. Within those categories, he outlined 23 "generally accepted styles" with descriptions.

I include them here to show how much the classification of beer styles has evolved.

Bottom-fermented

Bock—Strong, typically dark.

Doppelbock. Extra strong; by custom, brand names have the suffix *–ator*.

Dortmunder—Less hoppy than pilsner, drier than Munchener.

Munchener—Includes two types: dunkel (dark) and helles (golden).

Pilsner/Pilsener—Pale, golden, well-hopped.

Vienna—Amber-colored.

Wheat beers

Berliner weisse—Berlin's wheat beer, lighter than Weizenbier.

Gueuze-lambic—Brussels' spontaneously fermented wheat beer.

Weizenbier—Bavarian wheat beer.

Top-fermented

Alt—Dusseldorf's ale.

Bitter ale—Heavily hopped, copper-colored draft beer.

Bitter stout (Dublin)—Guinness is the definitive example.

Brown beers—Dark with subtle dry-sweet palate.

(Burton) Pale ale—Pale compared to porter, also known as India pale ale.

Kolsch—Pale, golden.

Mild ale—Lightly hopped, low-alcohol draft beer.

Milk stout—Low alcohol, faintly lactic, also known as sweet stout.

Porter—Modest-strength dark beer.

Russian stout.—Extra strong, comparable in strength to barley wine.

Saison—Naturally conditioned ale from the Belgian/French border.

Scotch ales—Ranging in strength from mild 54-shilling to wee heavy.

Steam beer—A hybrid between top and bottom fermented beer, associated with San Francisco.

Trappiste—Extra-strong, produced exclusively by abbeys in Belgium and the Netherlands.

Recommended reading

The essays in this book explore the background and flavors of 50 worldwide beer styles, from the lightest, palest ale to the deepest, darkest stout. Read them with a full pint in hand, and you'll soon find yourself reaching for even more.

For a more in-depth exploration, I recommend the following books and resources. Some are out of print but available through eBay and Amazon.

- *Michael Jackson's Beer Companion* by Michael Jackson (Running Press), 1993.

- *Tasting Beer* by Randy Mosher (Storey), 2009.

- *The Essential Styles* of Beer by Fred Eckhardt (Fred Eckhardt Communications), 1989.

- *The World Guide to Beer* by Michael Jackson (Running Press), 1977.

Additionally, detailed specifications of beer styles are maintained by and are available online from the Brewers Association and the Beer Judge Certification Program. Specifications from both organizations are included in this guide.

Finally, Brewers Publications offers an oustanding series of books dedicated to individual styles, from altbier to wild brews. They're especially good resources for brewers.

Jargon

I am a tabloid newspaper writer at heart, so you won't find much technical language in my writing. Sometimes, though, I slip into beer geek mode, and I apologize if I leave you behind.

Some terms to know before plowing forward.

abv—Alcohol by volume. The standard method of denoting strength in American beer today, largely replacing the older measurement of "alcohol by weight." When you hear someone talk about 3.2 beer, that usually refers to ABW. Today's standard lager clocks in around 4 percent abv; ale usually starts about 5 percent abv. Bock, India pale ale, porter, stout and other varieties may reach 10 percent abv and higher.

Adjuncts—Starch sources other than malted barley or wheat, such as corn, sugar and rice.

Ale and Lager—The two basic classifications of beer, differentiated by their method of yeast fermentation. Ale is fermented at a warm temperature (60-70 degrees) for a short period, with the yeast floating to the top. Lager is fermented at a cool temperature (under 50 degrees), with the yeast settling to the bottom.

Bottle-conditioning—Unfiltered beer that is bottled with additional yeast and sugar, to promote continued fermentation inside the bottle. This step produces natural carbon dioxide and enhances body. It sometimes leaves behind a small amount of sediment which is safe to d rink.

Craft beer—Beer made in small batches, typically without the use of adjuncts. Craft breweries are typically small businesses, though the big guys are increasingly producing gourmet brands (e.g. Blue Moon from Coors).

Dry hopping—The process of adding hops during fermentation to enhance aroma.

Fermentation—The process of yeast converting sugar into alcohol and carbon dioxide.

Finish—Flavor that lingers on the palate.

Grain—Mainly barley, but includes wheat, rye and other cereals.

Hops—The female flowers of the Humulus lupulus, or hop vine, used as a flavor, aroma and stability agent in beer.

IBUs—International bittering units. The measurement of a beer's bitterness, based on the level of alpha acid from hops.

Malt—A grain, usually barley, that is sprouted, then dried, roasted and crushed, used as the sugar source for yeast fermentation. Malt provides flavor and color.

Reinheitsgebot *(Rine-hites-ga-boat)*—The Bavarian beer purity law of 1516 that established only barley, water and hops could be used in the brewing of beer. After Louis Pasteur discovered the role of microorganisms in the process of fermentation in the 1860s, yeast was included as an acceptable ingredient.

Wort—The syrupy liquid extract from steeped grains that is fermented into beer.

The guide

Organizing so many beer styles was a bit of a challenge. Should I list them by alphabetical order? Style characteristics? Light to dark?

I drank a couple beers and chose none of the above.

Today's beers can be roughly divided into four very general categories: the Germans (mainly traditional lagers, including varieties from Bohemia and Austria), the English (mainly ales), the Belgians (often with distinctive yeast strains) and American extrapolations of those three.

That's how I've listed the styles in this guide. It may be overly simplistic and there's certainly room for argument. But that's what happens when you make decisions after drinking two or three pints of stout.

About the Checklists

In most cases, brands are named by brewery first.

Boldface brands are either benchmarks of the style or highly recommended.

Nearly all brands listed are available in bottles. Do yourself a favor: pour the beer into a glass. I've included suggested glassware for each style.

Unless country of origin is listed, checklist brands are brewed in America.

Because of the vagaries of beer importation and distribution, all beers may not be available in your hometown. Some of the beers are one-offs and may be extremely difficult to locate. If you can't find a specific brand, contact the brewery and ask the name of its brand wholesaler in your state. The wholesaler can help track down any of its brands.

Very few breweries will ship beer directly to you. Mail order companies fill that void, but there may be legal restrictions on shipping to your state.

Some websites, like BeerAdvocate.com, organize networks in which beer lovers trade bottles among themselves. It's a fun way to discover new flavors.

Otherwise, ask your friends—they're probably hiding something good in the back of the fridge.

The Germans

Altbier

There must be something wrong with *altbier*.

Some of America's best producers of the style barely acknowledge the name. Alaskan Brewing calls its version "Amber." At Otter Creek it's "Copper." And Long Trail just calls it "Strong Ale." You have to hunt for the small print on the neck label to learn the truth.

For years, Southampton Ales & Lagers called its altbier Secret Ale, as if its name couldn't be mentioned in mixed company.

"[Altbier] is hardly a marketable name," said Southampton brewer Phil Markowski. "If you do a straight interpretation, it just means 'old beer.'"

For the record, the "old" in altbier refers not to that ancient cardboard case buried under a layer of dust in the shadowy corner of your neighborhood distributor, but to its brewing technique. Much like you rejected your father's vinyl as yesterday's music, 19th-century Germany—hooked on new, crisp lagers—dismissed the heavy, dark ales made in Dusseldorf as "old."

Altbier, however, is not purely an ale, nor is it a lager. It is a hybrid.

It's classically made with the pale malts and Saaz hops of a typical German pilsner, some darker roasted grains and an aggressive, top-fermenting ale yeast that attenuates the wort completely to reduce the sweetness. Unlike an ale, however, it is fermented at cooler temps and conditioned for months, like a lager.

The result of this unusual brewing process is an entirely unique—and often underappreciated flavor.

Pour it into a traditional cylindrical glass, and as the foam reaches the rim, you get the welcoming aroma of malt and hops. The first swallow is followed by expected malty good-ness, but what's missing are the classic fruity esters produced by ale yeast. The hop bitterness is firm but not aggressive; instead of knocking you upside the head, it gently leads you to the clean, crisp finish of a lager.

Now, some will drain their glass and move onto something more challenging; they want more hops from their ale. That's why Markowski said it would be "simplistic" to call altbier a "German pale ale."

Others will take a big gulp and reach for the dreaded "D" word: drinkability. Smooth and dry, each sip encourages you to take another.

Unfortunately, "drinkability" has been co-opted by Bud Light to describe the total lack of flavor and body of its watered-down diet beer. Altbier — complex and beautifully balanced — deserves more than bland, patronizing praise.

Altbier

Aroma: Lightly malty, low hops.

Color: Copper or bronze.

Flavor: Some bitterness, but generally smooth with rich, biscuit-like malt.

Bitterness: 25-40 IBUs.

Strength: 4.5-6% abv.

"Altbier," said Markowski, "is a distinctive style. It has sort of a puzzling malty aroma, but in the classic versions it's noticeably bitter and clean. It has a broad appeal because it starts out malty and smooth. Then it has a bracing bitterness, but instead of a lingering hop flavor, it finishes clean and dry and makes you want to have another."

A beer this sublime deserves its own name! I'm pleased to report that Markowski came around recently and ditched his Secret Ale label. Today, it's proudly called Southampton Altbier.

Altbier Checklist

□ Alaskan Amber

□ Barre Alt (Germany)

□ Bluegrass Altbier

□ Diebels Alt (Germany)

□ Holsten Duckstein (Germany)

□ Erie Heritage Alt

□ Fordham Copperhead Ale

□ Füchschen Alt (Germany)

□ Frankenheim Alt

□ Grolsch Amber Ale (Netherlands)

□ Headless Man Amber Alt

□ Long Trail Double Bag

□ Ninkasi Sleigh'r Dark Doüble Alt

□ OMB Copper

□ Organic Münster Alt (Germany)

□ Otter Creek Copper Ale

□ Pinkus Original Alt (Germany)

□ Schmaltz's Alt

□ Schwelmer Alt (Germany)

□ Schumacher Alt (Germany)

□ Shonan Ruby (Japan)

□ Southampton Altbier

□ Tyranena Headless Man Amber Alt

□ **Uerige Doppelsticke** (Germany)

□ Uerige Sticke (Germany)

□ Widmer Okto

Berliner Weisse

I like my coffee black, my whiskey straight and my hefeweizen without a lemon. But I'm a total sucker for that green syrup they pour into Berliner Weisse.

It's called woodruff, made from a sweet, aromatic herb, and it's usually served as a dessert topping. How anyone thought to spike a wheat beer with something that is the approximate color of anticeptic mouthwash is beyond me. Yet, if you order a goblet in any Berlin beer garden, the waiter will almost surely ask: "*Rot oder grün?*" A *schuss* (or shot) of red or green?

The red is sweet raspberry syrup, which is kid stuff. The green gives the pale yellow beer the misty, grayish hue of a cloudy morning at the seashore. Not particularly attractive... but the syrup's cut-grass flavor softens and complements the beer's trademark tartness.

Not surprisingy, there's a bit of controversy surrounding the Syrup Question, and I'm not talking about red or green. So-called purists say you shouldn't add it at all. Mike Griffin, who authors the online British Guide to German Beer, says the syrup unnecessarily masks the intense character of Berliner Weisse

"If you're used to assertive flavours, such as Brussels Gueuze, Islay malt whiskies and spicy foods," he told me, "it really goes against the grain to put syrup in your beer. The syrup removes the beer's refreshing, distinctive qualities."

Like gueuze, the character of Berliner Weisse is produced by its intentional exposure to something most brewers normally would rather keep out of the fermentation tank. Where gueuze gets its funky barnyard aroma from the Brettanomyces strain of yeast, Berliner Weisse picks up its tartness from Lactobacillus, a type of bacteria that converts sugar into lactic acid.

"Without the bacteria," said Brandon Greenwood, the former brewer at Nodding Head in Philadelphia who created the brewpub's endearingly named Ich Bin Ein Berliner Weisse, "it's a boring, tasteless wheat beer. There are no hops to speak of and it doesn't have any of that banana or clove flavor from traditional wheat yeast."

With an acidity that Michael Jackson once described as "worthy of Dorothy Parker," Berliner Weisse is a challenging beer at first. "For those who aren't familiar with it, it's a bit of a shock," Greenwood said. "It's overwhelmingly tart on the first sip. But after that, the fruity esters come out on the palate, so you get a citrus kind of component."

What you also get is refreshment.

The tartness cleans the palate and slakes the thirst. Its low (3.5 percent abv) alcohol lets you drink it all afternoon without breaking into a sweat.

Berliner Weisse

Aroma: Sour, acidic with light fruit.

Flavor: Tart like lemonade with mild traces of grain.

Bitterness: 3-8 IBUs.

Strength : 2.5-4% abv.

The style probably dates to the 1500s and was so renowned that Napoleon's troops supposedly called it the "Champagne of the North." As late as the early 1900s more than 700 breweries produced it; today, however, it's bottled regularly only by two or three in Germany, including Kindl and Weihenstephan. Often, the version served in Berlin's beer gardens is closer to kiddie soda pop.

Surprisingly, authentic Berliner weisse has enjoyed a minor resurgence in the United States, mostly after Greenwood's draft version began picking up awards in the early 2000s. More than one American beer judge has told me that he or she now regards Nodding Head's as the style's benchmark.

So, I asked the expert: With our without a *schuss*?

"I would say the purists drink it neat and the recreational users add woodruff," Greenwood said. "I personally prefer it neat."

Berliner Weisse Checklist

☐ Bayerischer Bahnhof Berliner Style Weisse (Germany)

☐ Bell's Oarsman

☐ **Berliner Kindl Weisse** (Germany)

☐ Bethlehem Berliner Weisse

☐ Dogfish Head Fëstina Peche

☐ New Belgium Lips of Faith

☐ **Nodding Head Ich Bin Ein Berliner Weisse**

☐ Professor Fritz Briem 1809 Berliner Weisse (Germany)

☐ Southampton Berliner Weisse

☐ The Bruery Hottenroth

☐ White Birch Berliner Weisse

Bock

Imagine the scene:

The winter has ended, the sun is shining and the sidewalks are packed with milling crowds. Finely colored lithographs of playful billy goats raising foamy steins hang from the walls of every restaurant in town. A stream of beer trucks parades down the avenue. Celebrities judge a beauty pageant for goats in the city park. Brass bands play Strauss in outdoor gardens.

And a quarter million barrels of strong, dark, malty lager are about to be tapped across town.

Munich at its finest?

No, New York City, circa 1934.

It would be the first spring after the end of Prohibition, and—aside from the frantic days immediately after the enactment of the 21st Amendment four months earlier—this was perhaps America's grandest beer celebration:

The Return of Bock Beer.

The style—or, at least the name—is ancient, tracing its roots to the 15th-century northern Germany town of Einbeck (pronounced in the dialect of Bavaria as ein-*bock*.). "It is a delicious, famous and very palatable beverage and excellent beer," one German writer remarked in the 1500s, "wherewith a man, when partaken of in moderation, may save his health and his sound senses, and yet feel jolly and stimulated." The style evolved as a spring beer, brewed in the winter with extra malt and aged till it would be enjoyed during Lenten fasting — a tradition that continued as Germans emigrated across the Atlantic throughout the 19th century.

Absence makes the heart (and the palate) grow fonder. During Prohibition, grown men would rhapsodize about the aroma to their sons who'd grown up without even a whiff. Even non-drinkers mourned the loss of those ubiquitous goat posters (many of which are now part of a collection at the Library of Congress).

When March 1934 rolled around, American brewers were ready. A huge stockpile of bock had been brewed over the winter months, and the New York Brewers Board of Trade officially declared that the 15th would be Bock Day.

The New York Times and other newspapers, recognizing bock season as a cultural touchstone, published dozens of reports. There were contests and parades and goats—the traditional symbol of bock beer—grazing in Central Park. One of them, a black-bearded ruminant named Pretzels, was selected by a panel of well-known artists as "Mr. Bock Beer, 1934."

An astounding 250,000 barrels—equal to about 10 pints for every man, woman and child in New York City—would be delivered and drained within three weeks.

Bock

Aroma: Strong malty nose, no hops.

Flavor: Complex malt from decoction mash.

Bitterness: 20-30 IBUs.

Strength: 5-7.5% abv.

It was enough to put a smile on your face, even in the midst of the Great Depression. A bartender, explaining the appeal of bock, told one newspaper reporter simply, "It makes a feller feel good sooner."

The following year, the United States Brewers Association made plans to brew one billion bottles nationwide. Bock was back.

Unfortunately, it would be a short-lived return.

In 1942, patriotic brewers nationwide—citing the extra barley, trucks and gasoline required for the special lager— agreed they'd stock no bock until Hirohito and Hitler were defeated. When America emerged from the war, its fondness for dark beer had faded and bock was a shadow of its former self. The goats were still on the bottles and cans, but inside the alcohol content reached barely 5 percent by volume.

It would take the American microbrewery revolution to bring it back to its traditional strength, and even push its limits with increasingly more potent doppelbocks. But even with more than 1,500 separate varieties made in America today, bock is nowhere near as celebrated as it was in that hopeful spring of 1934.

Bock Checklist

- ☐ Aass Bock (Norway)
- ☐ Anchor Bock
- ☐ Bock Damm (Spain)
- ☐ Breckenridge Pandora's Bock
- ☐ Christoffel Bokbier (Netherlands)
- ☐ D' Inn'Staade (Germany)
- ☐ Deschutes Broken Top Bock
- ☐ Dreher Bak (Hungary)
- ☐ **Einbecker Ur-Bock Dunkel** (Germany)
- ☐ Genesee Bock
- ☐ Hofstettner Granitbock (Austria)
- ☐ Holsten Festbock (Germany)
- ☐ Italianao Bibock (Italy)
- ☐ Jopen Bokbier (Netherlands)
- ☐ Kneitinger Bock (Germany)
- ☐ La Trappe Bockbier (Netherlands)
- ☐ Left Hand Rye Bock
- ☐ Leinenkugel 1888 Bock
- ☐ Mahr's Christmas Bock (Germany)
- ☐ Michelob Amber Bock
- ☐ Millstream Schokolade Bock
- ☐ New Glarus Uff-da
- ☐ O'Fallon Goat's Breath
- ☐ Original Stieglbock (Austria)
- ☐ Paddock Wood Bock (Canada)
- ☐ Paper City Goats Peak
- ☐ Samuel Adams Winter Lager
- ☐ Saranac Black Diamond
- ☐ Schell's Bock
- ☐ Shiner Bock
- ☐ Sprecher Winter Brew
- ☐ Stegmaier Brewhouse Bock
- ☐ Stolichno Bock (Bulgaria)
- ☐ União Super Bock Stout (Portugal)
- ☐ Vyškov Jubiler (Czech)
- ☐ **Weltenburger Kloster Asam Bock** (Germany)
- ☐ Yuengling Bock

Bohemian Pilsner

After decades of callous abuse by megabrewers, it's no wonder pilsner gets such a bad rap from beer lovers. The aroma, the flavor, the body, the marvel—all have been sacrificed in the name of mass production.

I wretched the first time I read a highway billboard's bold declaration, "Miller Lite: True Pilsner."

True pilsner—Bohemian pilsner—is the single most glorious achievement in the entire history of beer. Its invention 165 years ago brought the world its first clear, golden lager, a new style that spawned a thousand imitators and revolutionized brewing forever. At its finest, pilsner is a delicate, refreshing glass with a pure, flowery bouquet and a crisp finish. True pilsner is the happy confluence of art and technology, of man striving to make himself better through his own ingenuity.

The world was a dark place in 1842. The British were at war with China. A cholera epidemic was spreading through Europe. And the city of Plzen, now part of the Czech Republic, was cursed with sour beer.

Mankind may never end war and disease, but it found a way to make better beer. The town hired a Bavarian to fix its problem. Like the brewers who preceded him, Josef Groll had the benefit of Bohemia's finest Saaz hops and its soft water. But he also had the advantage of a broadening array of 19th century technology:

- He traveled to England to learn the latest method of kilning to produce a lighter-colored malt.
- He made his wort with a decoction mash, a highly complex method in which the kettle temperature is raised in stages by removing a part of the mash and boiling it separately, then returning to the brew pot.

- He got his hands on a new strain of German lager yeast that would allow him to ferment the beer longer at a lower temperature without risking bacterial infection.
- He used new thermometers and hydrometers to help him perfect his methods.

The history bears repeating because the distinct flavor and quality of Bohemian pilsner is a product of all that emerging technology. The lighter malt gave us the golden color. Decoction brought out the malt flavor, but left its body smooth. The slower fermentation produced a clearer, crisper beer.

In later years the beauty of Groll's finished beer—now called Pilsner Urquell—would be enhanced by two more of the century's most important technological advances: cheap, mass-produced glassware and artificial refrigeration.

It was fully revolutionary.

The Germans, frightened by pilsner's new popularity, created their own variety, with a bigger hop bite. In America, Adolphus Busch developed another version (with rice) and called it Budweiser. Throughout the United States, "Bohemian" became synonymous with quality and excellence.

Dark ales would virtually disappear. Yellow beer was king.

Bohemian pilsner

Aroma: Spicy Saaz hops, light malt.

Flavor: Complex maltiness with a pronounced but not harsh hops presence, dry finish.

Bitterness: 35-45 IBUs.

Strength: 4.2-5.4% abv.

The glorious achievement would come full circle by the 21st century. Thanks to cheaper ingredients, duller tastes and crass advertising, pilsner would devolve into watered-down diet beer. Beer geeks snub them, few American craft brewers make them.

Sad, because this is a beer style that established the very notion of a definable beer style: it is a singularly recognizable product of technique, ingredients and environment. Cold, clean, aromatic, delicately hopped, golden, clear, refreshing and flavorful—that is a *true* Bohemian pilsner.

Bohemian Pilsner Checklist

☐ Creemore Springs Traditional Pilsner (Canada)

☐ Czechvar (Czech)

☐ Dock Street Bohemian Pilsner

☐ Golden Pheasant (Czech)

☐ Karlovacko (Croatia)

☐ Kláster Premium Lager (Czech)

☐ Krušovice Imperial (Czech)

☐ King Pilsner (Canada)

☐ Lagunitas Pils

☐ Lancaster Gold Star

☐ Měšťanský Rebel (Czech)

☐ Meteor Pils (France)

☐ Mikkeller Tjekket Pilsner (Denmark)

☐ New Glarus Two Women Lager

☐ Oskar Blues Mama's Little Yela Pils

☐ Otter Creek Vermont Lager

☐ **Pilsner Urquell** (Czech)

☐ Primator Premium Lager (Czech)

☐ Red Hook Rope Swing

☐ Samuel Adams Noble Pils

☐ Saranac Bohemian Pilsener

☐ Shiner 101

☐ Starobrno (Czech)

☐ Staropramen (Czech)

☐ Summit Pilsner

☐ Tuatara Pilsner (New Zealand)

☐ Velké Popovice Kozel (Czech)

☐ Žatec (Czech)

Dark Lager

If Al Gore is right, you've got to wonder what fans of rich, dark beer will be drinking in, oh, 2085.

It certainly won't be inky black imperial stout or high-octane barleywine—not when the afternoon high outside your infrared-shielded hut is 120 degrees in February.

Fizzy & yellow won't do, either—not unless your principled stance on drinking only quality, full-flavored beer melted along with the polar ice cap.

What will you drink when Boston is under water and you're sizzling like a Weber?

My guess: dark lager.

Rich, yes. Dark, obviously. But unlike many other ebony darlings, it's low in alcohol and never cloying. Instead of depending on huge grain bills for its color, traditional dark lager gets its depth from a smartly selected mix of caramel and roasted malt. You get the color and malty flavor without the added sugar or alcohol.

More importantly, you get a surprising mouthful of refreshment.

"If you blindfolded people and they couldn't see the color, they'd never know it was a dark beer," said Al Marzi, vice president of Harpoon's brewing operations who designed his brewery's superb Munich-Type Dark. "It's deceptive. You've got a pretty dark-looking beer, but when you taste it, it's much lighter on your palate than you'd expect." A well-made dark lager goes down as easily as a crystal-clear pilsner, but it is hardly delicate or flowery. Hops are in there, sure, but they're an undertone to the complexity of the malt. One gulp gives you a slight sweetness up front with a mild burnt bitterness in the afterglow, like popping roasted marshmallows at a campfire.

Brian O'Reilly, who brews Sly Fox Dunkel Lager in Royersford, Pa., believes the secret to dark lager is its yeast. "If you compare it to brown ale, dark lager is a little dryer," O'Reilly said. "Lager yeast doesn't produce any fruity esters, it has a real mellow nose."

Harpoon uses ale yeast, but Marzi said it's fermented at a low temperature to reduce the fruitiness.

Dark lager

Aroma: Rich malt sweetness, touch of chocolate.

Flavor: Medium body, rich malt sweetness, low hops, hints of chocolate, caramel.

Bitterness: 18-28 IBUs.

Strength: 4.5—5.6% abv.

Both versions are purely refreshing and flush down easily.

I know, dark beer in the raging heat sounds counterintuitive … till you look at some of the classic brews coming out of hot-weather countries: Xinghu from Brazil, Alahambra Negra from Spain and San Miguel Dark from the Philippines. And Mexico? Forget lime-infused Corona. Everyone knows the most flavorful, refreshing mainstream beer from south of the border is Negra Modelo.

All of those darks take their cues from the originals made, of course, in Germany. Years before the world fell in love with yellow lager, it was dark brown that filled the steins in Munich's beer gardens. Gabriel Sedlmayer II of the Spaten brewery gets credit for perfecting the style, sometime in the 1840s, and it remained Bavaria's most popular style for the next 50 years. These days, it's regarded by many as "old-fashioned," but you can still hear the lederhosen crowd yell for "dunkels" at Hofbrauhaus.

In the United States, unfortunately, dark lager is a niche style, possibly because hairy-chested fans of big, dark stouts and warming double bocks find it too thin while light lager drinkers are scared off by its color.

But we are facing a climate crisis. It's time to seek out innovative solutions. Dark lager just might be the official beer of global warming.

Dark Lager Checklist

- ☐ Alahambra Negra (Spain)
- ☐ Baltika #4 Original (Russia)
- ☐ Beck's Dark
- ☐ Beerlao Dark (Laos)
- ☐ Budvar Dark Lager (Czech)
- ☐ Černá Hora Granát (Czech)
- ☐ **Dinkel Acker Dark** (Germany)
- ☐ Dixie Blackened Voodoo
- ☐ Efes Dark (Turkey)
- ☐ Eggenberg Dark Lager (Czech)
- ☐ Fischer Tradition Amber (France)
- ☐ Guinness Black Lager (Ireland)
- ☐ Heineken Dark Lager (Netherlands)
- ☐ Jacobsen Dark Lager (Denmark)
- ☐ Kozel Dark (Czech)
- ☐ Layla Dirty Blonde (Israel)
- ☐ Lev Black Lion (Czech)
- ☐ Mac's Black Mac (Australia)
- ☐ Matilda Bay Dogbolter (Australia)
- ☐ McSorley's Irish Black Lager
- ☐ Moerlein Barbarossa Double Dark Lager
- ☐ Negra Modelo (Mexico)
- ☐ Pietra (France)
- ☐ Saranac Chocolate Amber Lager
- ☐ Zagrebacka Tomislav Pivor (Croatia)
- ☐ Žatec Xantho (Czech)

Munich Dunkel Lager Checklist

- ☐ Ayinger Altbairish Dunkel (Germany)
- ☐ Capital Dark
- ☐ Eisenbahn Escura (Brazil)
- ☐ Ettaler Kloster Dunkel (Germany)
- ☐ Felsenau Bärni Dunkel (Switzerland)
- ☐ Flensburger Dunkel (Germany)
- ☐ Gösser Dark (Austria)
- ☐ Harpoon Munich-Type Dark Beer
- ☐ Hofbräu Dunkel (Germany)
- ☐ König Ludwig Dunkel (Munich)
- ☐ Mother Earth Dark Cloud
- ☐ Ostfriesen Bräu Landbier Dunkel (Germany)
- ☐ Saranac Lake Effect
- ☐ Schell's Dark
- ☐ Schönram Altbairish Dunkel (Germany)
- ☐ Sly Fox Dunkel Lager
- ☐ Spaten Dunkel (Germany)
- ☐ Victory Dark Lager
- ☐ Warsteiner Premium Dunkel (Germany)
- ☐ Weihenstephaner Tradition (Germany)
- ☐ **Weltenburger Barock Dunkel** (Germany)

Eisbock

nd now for some basic physical science.

- Freezing temperature of water: **0 °C.**
- Freezing temperature of pure ethanol: **-114 °C.**

OK, Mr. Science, let's see what happens when you submit a batch of, say, potent double bock to sub-zero temperatures. Like magic, the beer's dissolved ions of alcohol separate from the H_2O.

The de-alcoholized liquid, with its higher freezing temperature, moves to the surface and the sides of the tank where it's coldest and solidifies. The dense remainder of malty solids and concentrated alcohol collects at the center, where it can be racked away from the ice to complete a process known as "freeze distillation."

At least, that's what you'd call it that if you wore a white lab coat and Coke bottle glasses.

Everyone else knows it as eisbock.

Thick, oily and boozy, this style may at first seem like a laboratory experiment gone wrong, as if the brewer had been assisted by Igor and his pal Abby Normal. Dive into the waft of bracing alcohol and you can't help but wonder: Is this beer or a genetic misfit? The numbing warmth will put a smile on your face and have you checking the side of the bottle for the abv. Nine percent... ten percent... One of the best known, Schneider Avent-inus Weizen Eisbock, nails 12, while the occasional brewpub has reached all the way to 18 percent alcohol.

Yet, like a good whisky, a well-made eisbock is hardly one dimensional.

A beakerful may be as sweet as honey, with a fruity (plum or raisin) twist. Kulmbacher Reichelbräu Eisbock seems nutty, like caramel-covered almonds. Schloss Eggenberg Urbock Dunkel Eisbock is surprisingly smooth with light herbal notes.

With its strong character, eisbock is a beer that deserves a minute or two of contemplation. In the glow of the afterburn, the irony begins to sink in, that this most warming of beer styles is the product of a deep chill.

The German breweries that perfected eisbock like to share tall tales of how they discovered this beer by accident. There is, for example, the 19th-century story passed along by the German Beer Institute of the mistakenly frozen casks of bock at the old Reichelbräu brewery in Kulmbach. An unfortunate "brewery lad" got the blame and was forced to crack open the wooden casks and lap up the pool of "murky, brownish liquid." The dazed kid, the story goes, was the "first human" to taste eisbock.

Eisbock
Aroma: Strong malt with a huge alcohol presence.
Flavor: Sweet, with an extreme, complex malt character that may reveal fruit, nut or honey notes.
Bitterness: 25-30 IBUs.
Strength: 9% abv—the sky's the limit.

Maybe there's some truth here, but the fact is man has been suffering from frozen beer ever since God invented February. Page through history books, and you'll find dreary stories of lost sailors starving in the northern reaches of the Atlantic, desperately chipping away at frozen casks before succumbing to cannibalism. (An icy brown ale paired with a severed limb, perhaps?)

Sometimes, yesteryear's brewers iced their beer on purpose. Before the British invented India pale ale to survive those long voyages to Asia, the Tasmanians actually froze their highly regarded beer into solid blocks before shipping it throughout the South Pacific. Similarly, colonial American brewers froze hard apple cider to create an 80 proof delight called applejack.

At this point, it's probably necessary to warn: Do not confuse eisbock with North American ice beer. The latter is an abomination, in which, after freezing, the lifeless lager is weakened with the addition of water.

Eisbock, by contrast, is a marvel of science.

Eisbock Checklist

Note: Because U.S. law prohibits the brewimg of traditional eisbock (it is considered a form of distillation), American versions of the style are rare.

☐ Baron Seven Swabians Eisbock

☐ Kiuchi Commemorative Ale (Japan)

☐ Kronenbrauerei Söflingen Natureisbock Hell (Germany)

☐ Kuhnhenn Winter Wonder Lager

☐ Kulmbacher Reichelbräu Eisbock (Germany)

☐ L'Alchimiste Eisbock (Canada)

☐ Nordbräu Ingolstadt Eisbock (Germany)

☐ Ramstein Winter Wheat Eisbock

☐ Red Hook Eisbock 28

☐ Schloss Eggenberg Urbock Dunkel Eisbock (Austria)

☐ **Schneider Aventinus Weizen Eisbock** (Germany)

☐ Schorschbräu Schorschbock 40% (Germany)

☐ SNAB Ijsbok (Belgium)

☐ Southampton Double Ice Bock

☐ Vancouver Island Hermannator Ice Bock (Canada)

German Pils

Did you happen to catch the New York Times a while back when writer Eric Asimov complained about the lousy beer selection (nine bucks for a single can of PBR!) at Yankee Stadium? Where, he wondered, were the authentic pilsners?

Not those watery mainstream poseurs (I'm talking to you, Miller Lite) that claim to possess "true" pilsner flavor. Asimov wondered about the whereabouts of a style that seems designed for a long afternoon in the grandstands—crisp, refreshing, light-bodied with an assertive hoppy bitterness and an exceptionally dry finish.

One hundred miles south of the Bronx, fans of the Philadelphia Phillies could only chuckle when Asimov listed his top 10 American pilsners. Three of them—Troegs Sunshine Pils, Victory Prima Pils and Sly Fox Pikeland Pils—are among the popular crafts on tap at the Phils' ballpark.

Indeed, the southeastern corner of Pennsylvania has emerged as a hotbed of craft-brewed pilsners. In one tiny 40-mile triangle just outside of Philly, Victory, Sly Fox and Stoudt's Brewing have amassed a dozen pilsner medals at the Great American Beer Festival.

The region is known especially for its German-style pils, and more precisely northern German.

The distinction is obvious when comparing two classics from the south and north, Spaten from Munich and Jever from near the sea. Both are bright and clear and golden, the product of pale malts and aromatic Hallertau hops. These are fine sons of the style born in Bohemia in 1842 (see page 28).

Raise each glass to your mouth and the difference emerges quickly. Spaten's hops are softly aromatic and its malt is bready; Jever seems ready to punch you in the nose. Take a sip, and the Bavarian caresses you with a sweet, mellow kiss. The stark Teuton from the north bites you on the tongue.

Same country, same style, two different beers.

Blame it on the water. In the north, it's naturally hard with calcium, which highlights hop bitterness, especially the somewhat metallic Tettnanger variety.

Which hardly explains the popularity of German pils in the Keystone State.

For that, you might look to Stoudt's, the state's first microbrewery whose pilsner came to define the American variety of craft-brewed pilsner. In a five-year span in the mid-1990s, Stoudt's Pils won three golds and a bronze at the GABF. (It's no coincidence that one of the early mentors of Stoudt's brewers was Karl Strauss, born at a brewery in northern Germany.)

"Stoudt's set the standard for doing German lagers," said Brian O'Reilly, brewmaster at Sly Fox Brewing in Royersford, Pa., whose pilsners have won three GABF medals. "Then Victory came along with Prima Pils, and now people in this region are just used to the flavor."

Victory's German-trained co-founder Bill Covaleski credits Stoudt's too, but looks back a bit further. The region, he

German Pils

Aroma: Light malt with spicy hops and mild sulfur.

Flavor: Crisp, bitingly bitter

Bitterness: 25-45 IBUs.

Strength: 4.5—5.5% abv.

notes, was largely settled by Germans; the Pennsylvania Dutch still farm the acres of Chester and Lancaster counties just to the west of Victory's brewery in Downingtown, Pa.

"Pils never went away in this area," said Covaleski. "We never lost our taste for it... I remember when I was 10 years old, tasting my dad's Carling Black Label. It was harsh and bitter just like a German pils."

Carling Black Label? I think that's on tap at Yankee Stadium.

German Pils Checklist

- ☐ Abita S.O.S.
- ☐ Bavaria Pilsener (Netherlands)
- ☐ Bavik Pils (Belgium)
- ☐ Bitburger (Germany)
- ☐ Bohemia (Mexico)
- ☐ Brooklyn Pilsner
- ☐ Christoffel Blond (Netherlands)
- ☐ Dinkel Acker Pils (Germany)
- ☐ Efes Pilsener (Turkey)
- ☐ EKU Pils (Germany)
- ☐ Flensburger Pilsener (Germany)
- ☐ **Jever Pilsener** (Germany)
- ☐ Knappstein Reserve Lager (Australia)
- ☐ König Pilsener (Germany)
- ☐ Left Hand Polestar Pilsner
- ☐ New Belgium Blue Paddle
- ☐ North Coast Scrimshaw Pilsner
- ☐ Paulaner Premium Pils (Germany)
- ☐ Pinkus Organic Ur Pils (Germany)
- ☐ Radeberger Pilsner (Germany)
- ☐ Rogue Über Pils
- ☐ Rothaus Tannenzäpfle (Germany)
- ☐ Saint Arnold Summer Pils
- ☐ Saranac Adirondack Lager
- ☐ Schell's Pilsner
- ☐ Sly Fox Pikeland Pils
- ☐ Spaten Pils (Germany)
- ☐ Stoudt's Pils
- ☐ Sudwerk Pilsner
- ☐ Troegs Sunshine Pils
- ☐ Trumer Pils
- ☐ Tuppers' Hop Pocket Pils
- ☐ Veltins Pilsner (Germany)
- ☐ **Victory Prima Pils**
- ☐ Warsteiner Verum (Germany)
- ☐ Vitzthum Einhundert 100 Bitterpils (Austria)

Helles

Pale, yellow lager...*yawn*. It's as ordinary as white boxer shorts.

Try telling that to the Munich brewers who gathered a few weeks after their beloved Oktoberfest in 1895 to gripe about this newfangled brew called Helles Lagerbier. That kind of talk would have had you facing the wrath of Hans and Fritz, perhaps wearing those pointy *Pickelhauben* helmets, clicking their heels and railing about the purity of their dunkel beer.

"I take the view," spouted the owner of the Augustiner Brewery, as wonderfully related by the Bavarian Brewers Federation, "that the reputation of Munich beers has been greatly damaged by the brewing of pale beers, which has done nothing but to serve as an unnecessary advertisement for Pilsner beers."

Ah, yes, those blasted Pilsners, the plague of the Bohemians. Heading toward the 20th century, the crisp, refreshing golden lager was filling glasses in cafes across Europe. The Germans—traditionalists to a fault—believed at first that it was a passing fad. All they had to do was stand together, ignore the threat from the east, continue brewing their dark, fuller-bodied beers that generations of Munich brewers had perfected over three centuries.

But the ranks broke. In 1889, Eugen and Ludwig Thomas, both of whom had trained in Pilsen, had begun pouring something called Thomas-Hell ("hell" is German for "bright"). In the summer of '95, Spaten—the famed brewery of Gabriel Sedlmayr, the man who invented amber Oktoberfestbier—began pouring its own Helles Lagerbier.

This "unnecessary advertisement," of course, would become its own, distinct style—one that would emerge as the world's most popular.

Munich Helles, at first glance, is almost identical to Pilsner. Clear and blond they both sparkle with carbonation that rises to a creamy, white collar of foam. On a hot and muggy day, you just want to dive in and soak it up.

But a whiff and a swallow says you've got something different. Where Pilsner bites your tongue with the spice of Saaz hops, Helles fill your mouth with soft, mellow malt. Tettnang, Hallertau—they're in there, but only for balance not bitterness, for Munich's water does harsh things to hops. The finish is slightly sweet but certainly not cloying. It would be hard to find a more perfectly balanced beer.

Indeed, around the world, breweries have mimicked the style, often with palate-numbing results. Miller, Beck's, Singha, Corona,

Helles

Aroma: Clean and sweet with light hops.

Flavor: Somewhat sweet and malty, soft, very clean and refreshing.

Bitterness: 16-22 IBUs.

Strength: 4.7-5.4% abv

Molson, Red Stripe—they're all basically dumbed-down Helles, bright and crisp and balanced, yes, but with little distinctive character. Kind of like those white boxer shorts.

You want to know what an authentic Munich-style Helles taste like, you need to enjoy it on tap or from a fresh bottle from a brewery that you can trust not to screw it up with corn or industrial shortcuts. A perfect Helles—say, Weihenstephaner Original or Penn Gold—is rich and slightly bready, clean and smooth. You know you've got one in your hand when each sip urges you to take another.

Take a long pull, and consider the events of November 1895.

Looking back, you could say that those recalcitrant brewers were simply out of step with the world's changing tastes, that their uber-traditionalism—still predominant in the 21st century—has stunted German beer culture, that the insistence of hewing to centuries-old brewing guidelines has allowed other countries—Belgium, America, even Italy—to grab the spotlight with new, exotic styles, that without progress, you die.

Or you could say, dammit, if only the Munich brewers had stood strong, we might have been spared the scourge of Michelob Ultra.

Helles Checklist

- ☐ 7 Stern Wiener Helles (Austria)
- ☐ Altenmünster Metzger Helles (Germany)
- ☐ Altstadthof Helles (Germany)
- ☐ Atwater Hell Pale Lager
- ☐ **Augustiner Bräu Edelstoff** (Germany)
- ☐ Ayinger Jahrhundert Bier (German)
- ☐ Barons Lager (Australia)
- ☐ Borbecker Helles Dampfbier (Germany)
- ☐ Cisco Summer of Lager
- ☐ Climax Hoffmann Helles
- ☐ Der Hirschbrau Neuschwansteiner (Germany)
- ☐ Ettaler Kloster Edelhell (Germany)
- ☐ Great Lakes Dortmunder Gold
- ☐ Hacker-Pschorr Münchner Gold (Germany)
- ☐ Löwenbräu Original (Germany)
- ☐ Maui Bikini Blonde Lager
- ☐ Mecklenburger Bavarian Lager

- ☐ Moerlein Lager House Original Golden Helles
- ☐ Moosbacher Lager (Germany)
- ☐ Paulaner Original (Germany)
- ☐ Rosengarten Einsiedler Lager Hell (Switzerland)
- ☐ Saranac Helles
- ☐ Shiner 99
- ☐ Smoky Mountain Velas Helles
- ☐ Spaten Munchner Hell (Germany)
- ☐ St. George Lager
- ☐ Stiegl Goldbräu (Austria)
- ☐ **Stoudt's Gold**
- ☐ Thomas Hooker Munich Style Golden Lager
- ☐ Three Floyds Gorch Fock Helles
- ☐ Victory Lager
- ☐ Weihenstephaner Original (Germany)
- ☐ Weltenburger Barock-Hell (Germany)

Kristallweizen

Kristall weiss: *A filtered version of hefeweizen.*

If that definition doesn't just make your skin crawl, well, you are a cold, heartless turtle. Why would anyone intentionally take one of the world's most-treasured beer styles—a variety whose unique beauty is in its murky, *unfiltered* body—and intentionally "cleanse" it? It's as if a brewery imagined that it could improve a Czech pilsner recipe by removing the hops and adding corn or rice…

On second thought… never mind. What one man calls castration, the advertising department calls "Great Taste! Less Filling!"

The good news is that, even without all that cloudy yeast and wheat sediment, crystal-clear kristall weiss still offers much of the signature aroma and flavor of a German wheat beer. It's the inevitable product of wondrous yeast activity that, at high fermentation temperatures, produces fruity esters and that famously clove-like phenol, 4-vinyl guaiacol. Banana, bubblegum, citrus—it all rises in a plume above the beer's billowing white head of foam.

Plant your nose into a glass of Bavarian-made Weihenstephaner, one of the more widely available kristallweizen in America, and you'll come out with the spring-like aroma of grapes and vanilla.

It's in the body where you'll notice the big difference between hefeweizen and a kristall weiss. Where the former boasts the healthy, creamy texture of wheat, the latter is crisply carbonated in a lager kind of way. The flavor is full and—with low hops—the finish is juicy, not dry. It's exceptionally clean and refreshing, like a reluctant lawnmower beer.

Most of the difference in body is a product of filtering, of course. Further, without all those suspended yeast nutrients, kristallweizen—unlike its unfiltered big brother—can not be bottle-conditioned. Now, I'm not going to sit here and tell you I can tell the difference between natural and artificial bubbles. But I will say that the clear beer seems to lose its head—its most appealing characteristic—a lot more quickly.

Deflated, a 10-minute-old kristall weiss looks like an ex- at your 20th high school reunion. What did you ever see in that loser?

Which brings us to the infamous lemon.

Having caponized their hefeweizen, Germans—at least the Deiters from the north—will actually plunk a slice into kristallweizen. Perhaps it's penance, or a feeble attempt to replace some of the lost character. Either way, the fruit has the unfortunate side effect of speeding along the foam's demise.

The cure, according to numerous sources, is to drop a few grains of rice into kristallweizen, which supposedly provide a surface for the formation of more CO_2 bubbles. Dubious, I tried the trick once.

The rice fell to the bottom, then floated up, then back down, and through close examination I can authoritatively

Kristalweizen

Aroma: Wheat and grass notes, clove and fruit, light hop character.

Flavor: Straw flavors, balanced with hops, citrus and spice.

Bitterness: 10-20 IBUs.

Strength: 4.5-5.5% abv.

report it was directly responsible for the magical creation of precisely 7 bubbles. Then, having forgotten the experiment, I continued drinking, till…

Well, let's just say this is where adulteration of a perfectly good wheat beer gets you. First they filter it, then you add rice, and then you're writhing on the floor with something stuck in your throat, vowing revenge on an entirely innocent kristall weiss.

Kristalweizen Checklist

- ☐ Allgäuer Fürstabt Kristallweizen (Germany)
- ☐ Bayern Dancing Trout Ale
- ☐ Bischoff Falkensteiner Weizen (Germany)
- ☐ Blue Mountain Rockfish Wheat
- ☐ Cascade Blonde (Australia)
- ☐ Eder & Heylands Bavaria Kristall Weizen (Germany)
- ☐ Eichbaum Kristall Weizen (Germany)
- ☐ Erdinger Weissbier Kristallklar (Germany)
- ☐ Farny Kristall-Weizen (Germany)
- ☐ Franziskaner Kristall Klar (Germany)
- ☐ Fürstenberg Weizen Kristallklar (Germany)
- ☐ Ganter Badisch Weizen Kristallklar (Germany)
- ☐ Gold Ochsen Weizenbier Kristall (Germany)
- ☐ Hacker-Pschorr Kristall Weisse (Germany)
- ☐ Harpoon Crystal Wheat
- ☐ Herrnbräu Kristall-Weizen (Germany)
- ☐ Hütt Weizen Kristall (Germany)
- ☐ Kaltenhausen Edelweiss Kristallklar Weissbier (Germany)
- ☐ Kulmbacher Kapuziner Kristall-Weizen (Germany)
- ☐ Leinenkugel's Honey Weiss
- ☐ Maisel's Weisse Kristall (Germany)
- ☐ Matilda Bay Redback Original (Australia)
- ☐ Memminger Kristallweizen (Germany)
- ☐ Paulaner Weissbier Kristallklar (Germany)
- ☐ Saint Arnold Texas Wheat
- ☐ Schneider Weisse Kristall (Germany)
- ☐ Schöfferhofer Kristallweizen (Germany)
- ☐ Spanish Peaks Crystal Weiss
- ☐ Tucher Kristall Weizen (Germany)
- ☐ **Weihenstephaner Kristall Weissbier** (Germany

Maibock

Sitting alone and quaffing the most widely sold maibock brewed in America, the daydreamer can't help but drift toward a quagmire of imponderables. Like:

- Exactly what's the difference between a Maibock and a Helles Bock.

And:

- Is Maibock, as even the normally unequivocal sages at the Beer Judges Certification Program ruminate in their darkest hours, a pale version of a traditional bock or a Munich Helles lager brewed to bock strength?

And, more immediately:

- How can Rogue say this delicious glass of Dead Guy Ale that I'm about to finish is a Maibock when it's called an ale? Last time I looked, a bock was a lager.

Why do I agonize over such things? I need to be more like Dan Gordon, the renowned California lager brewer. The first time he tasted Maibock, he was an exchange student sitting outside of his dormitory in the university town of Göttingen in Northern Germany, enjoying the finest from the nearby brewing town of Einbeck.

"I loved it immediately," Gordon said. "I never had anything like it before. It's a very unique style, and only two or three breweries were making it at the time."

He took a day off from schoolwork for a tour of the Einbecker brewery and firmly decided, "This is what I want to do with the rest of my life."

No doubts, no questions, no mundane worries about the stylistic heritage of this luscious glass of strong, pale German lager. Gordon enrolled at the famous brewing school at Weihenstephan, got himself a job and launched what would become one of the world's most successful brewpub chains, the Gordon Biersch Brewery Restaurant Group.

"Without Maibock," Gordon said, "there wouldn't be a Gordon Biersch."

I like that story: uncomplicated, certain.

Which is the best way to answer some of those questions that nag me from time to time, like:

- The difference between Maibock and Helles Bock? None, other than the former is what we call the latter when the calendar pages turn to Spring. It's a fitting lager for the changing seasons, stiff enough to shake winter chills,

Maibock

Aroma: Bready or toasted, with no apparent hops.

Flavor: Rich malt flavor in a medium body, mild sweetness with a bite of hops in the finish.

Bitterness: 20-35 IBUs.

Strength: 6-7.5% abv.

yet refreshing enough for the season's first go-round with the lawnmower. Brewed with Pils malts and balanced with distinctive Noble hops, its pale color seems a harbinger of the ice-cold lagers that we'll be cracking open after Memorial Day.

And:

- A light bock or a heavy Helles? It's a black hole, like asking if the glass is half empty or half full. Don't go there.

Which brings us to:

My now-empty glass of Dead Guy. How can Rogue say it's made "in the style of a German Maibock" when they acknowledge that it's fermented with the brewery's famous Pacman ale yeast?

The last swallow from my glass is why it's not worth troubling ourselves with imponderables.

Like any decent Maibock, Dead Guy fills the mouth with a toasty, caramel flavor. Not too heavy, not too light; sweet with bready malt, but never cloying; creamy yet refreshing with a crisp, slightly bitter finish. Finish one pint and you'll want another.

As Dan Gordon himself discovered, it's the flavor and drinkability that are so appealing in this style. Drink up and stop asking so many questions.

Maibock Checklist

- ☐ Abita Mardi Gras Bock
- ☐ Ahornberger Maibock (Germany)
- ☐ Allersheimer Maibock (Germany)
- ☐ Altenmünster Maibock (Germany)
- ☐ Andechser Bergbock Hell (Germany)
- ☐ Baeren Maibock (Germany)
- ☐ Bauhöfer Ulmer Maibock (Germany)
- ☐ Berkshire Maibock Lager
- ☐ Boulevard Boss Tom's Golden Bock
- ☐ Capital Maibock
- ☐ Dundee Pale Bock
- ☐ Einbecker Mai-Urbock (Germany)
- ☐ Erie Golden Fleece Maibock
- ☐ Flying Dog Heller Hound Bock Beer
- ☐ Foothills Gruffmeister Maibock
- ☐ Gordon Biersch Maibock
- ☐ Hoepfner Maibock (Germany)
- ☐ Hofbräu Maibock (Germany)
- ☐ Hofmark Engel Bock (Germany)
- ☐ Holsten Maibock (Germany)
- ☐ Klosterbräu Maibock Hell (Germany)
- ☐ Lakefront Big Easy Imperial Maibock
- ☐ **Lancaster Rumspringa**
- ☐ **Mahr's Bock** (Germany)
- ☐ Millstream Maifest
- ☐ Náchod Primátor Maibock (Czech)
- ☐ New Glarus Cabin Fever Bock
- ☐ Rahr Bucking Bock
- ☐ Ramstein Maibock
- ☐ Rogue Dead Guy Ale
- ☐ Samichlaus Helles (Austria)
- ☐ Schell Maifest
- ☐ **Sierra Nevada Glissade**
- ☐ Smuttynose Maibock
- ☐ Sprecher Mai Bock
- ☐ Stevens Point Einbock
- ☐ Stoudt's Blonde Double Maibock
- ☐ Summit Maibock
- ☐ Trader Joe's Hofbrau Bock
- ☐ Ulmer Maibock (Germany)
- ☐ Victory St. Boisterous

Rauchbier

I've got a beer-drinking buddy who's an absolute Luddite.

To him, progress did nothing but ruin the flavor of beer. Aluminum kegs, artificial CO-2, refrigeration and bottles—he sneers at it all while he sucks down pints of room-temperature, cask-conditioned ale that's been hand-pumped from oaken firkins.

And don't get him started on Louis Pasteur.

But pass him a glass of rauchbier and he whines like a baby: "Too smoky."

Too smoky? Yo, pal, before the 1700s, that's the way most beer tasted. Unless it was laid out on straw under the warm sun, malt was typically dried in wood-fired kilns that imparted a distinctive smoky aroma and flavor. And it could be nasty. One often-cited 18th-century beer guide noted that in some parts of England, "their malt is so stenched with the Smoak of the Wood, with which 'tis dryed, that no Stranger can endure it, though the inhabitants, who are familiarized to it, can swallow it…"

Technological progress gave us coal- and gas-fired furnaces, indirectly heated kilns and beer that didn't taste like a carton of Chesterfields. Rauchbier should've gone the way of buggy whips and Windows 95.

And, yet, some brewers still insist on smoking. Alaskan Brewing makes a popular smoked porter, Rogue brews a smoked ale and you'll get at least a whiff of smoke from many Scottish ales.

But the classic style of smoke is Bamberg's rauchbier (*rauch* is German for smoke).

Seven breweries operate in the baroque Franconian city north of Bavaria, but only two—Spezial and Heller-Trum—regularly produce rauchbier. The latter's Aecht Schlenkerla labels, which have become the benchmark of the style, are available in America. But for a better waft, head over to the brewery's 600-year-old tavern on Dominikanerstrasse and enjoy the smoke in half-liters served up from wooden kegs.

While Schlenkerla produces a bock, a weizen and a helles, it's the Märzen that will asphyxiate your senses to the fullest. Plunge your nose into a glass and you're greeted with a smoky aroma layered over a rich, strong malt base. A frothy glass is liquid Westphalian ham, reminiscent of an afternoon of schussing around in a pile of smoldering leaves. It'll take two to wash down a pork knuckle, a third to douse a stuffed Bamberg onion slathered with bacon and beer sauce.

Quality malt is the essence of a true rauchbier, said Victory Brewing's Bill Covaleski, whose Scarlet Fire is as close as any American brewer has come to the Bamberg original. "The real key in getting it right is keeping the hops in check," he said. "You don't want the hops to overwhelm the malt in any way."

Schlenkerla smokes its own malt, going through cord upon cord of seasoned Beechwood at its brewery. Homebrewers

Rauchbier
Aroma: Smoke varies from light to intense, with roasted malt.
Flavor: Malty with various levels of smoke, light hops.
Bitterness: 20-30 IBUs.
Strength: 4.8-6.5% abv.

can do it themselves, too, with a few chunks of hardwood and a Weber grill.

In an inevitable nod toward progress, however, American craft brewers usually turn to a malt supplier. Several produce a modern variety that is pre-stenched, as my drinking buddy might say, with the Smoak of the Wood.

Rauchbier Checklist

□ 3 Ravens Dark (Australia)

□ Aecht Schlenkerla Rauchbier Fastenbier (Germany)

□ Aecht Schlenkerla Rauchbier Urbock (Germany)

□ Aecht Schlenkerla Rauchbier Weizen (Germany)

□ Aecht Schlenkerla Eiche Doppelbock (Germany)

□ **Aecht Schlenkerla Rauchbier Märzen** (Germany)

□ Alaskan Smoked Porter

□ Caldera Rauch Ür Bock

□ Dark Horse Fore Smoked Stout

□ East End Smokestack Heritage Porter

□ Eisenbahn Rauchbier (Brazil)

□ Emelisse Rauchbier (Netherlands)

□ Flying Dog Dog Schwarz

□ Fort Collins Z Lager

□ Göller Rauchbier (Germany)

□ Left Hand Smoke Jumper

□ Rauchenfelser Steinbrau (Germany)

□ Rouget De Lisle Vieux Tuyé (France)

□ Samuel Adams Bonfire Rauchbier

□ Saranac Rauchbier

□ Sierra Nevada Rauchbier

□ Spezial Rauchbier Lager (Germany)

□ Trois Mosquetaires Rauchbier (Canada)

□ Victory Scarlet Fire

□ Viking Rauch

□ Weiherer Rauch (Germany

Weizenbock

This insidious practice of cramming a cheap rind of lemon atop a luscious, aromatic glass of hefeweizen—the taproom equivalent of slobbering ketchup all over a perfectly grilled T-bone from Morton's—has got to stop. But, as I am in no position to halt rampant half-wittedness, I urge you to fight fire with fire, or more accurately, wheat with wheat.

No one would dare defile a weizenbock.

It is dark and moody and will bite your head off if you make it wear that silly hat.

Order it instead of the hefe the next time you see it on draft, but be prepared to wait. The spigot invariably gushes mounds of foam, no matter how much the bartender tilts the glass. She'll let it sit, return to fill again, let it sit... it makes the wait for a properly poured pint of Guinness seem like snap.

A weizenbock is, at its heart, a German wheat beer, only more so.

You get the drift when at last you raise the glass to your nose. The aromatic esters are there—the banana, the clove, the bubble gum you love in a hefeweizen. It's probably the same yeast strain, just pulling double duty at the brewery.

But it's a bock, remember, and not because someone figured how to make a bottom-fermenting wheat beer. No, this is still an ale; the bock here is all about muscle: more wheat malt, more barley and, yeah, more alcohol.

So as your weizenbock seduces you with its perfume, it's filling your mouth with a bold array of flavor: doughy bread, ripe fruit, candied spice, maybe a hint of chocolate. Don't hunt around for the hops, they're only there to offset the sweetness. Go ahead, suck her down and try to sort it all out. But by the time you hit bottom, you're going to forget what the question was. Eight percent alcohol has a funny way of barging into the room and changing the subject.

What is this beer, a temptress or a brute?

The answer is in the fermentation.

With that big time malt bill, an ale has a tendency to go off on the brewer, bubbling madly till he's left with too much octane and too little body. Worse, it's alcohol of the fusel variety, the kind that gives you headaches of biblical proportions. Slow it down by dropping the temperature, and he risks losing those lovely esters that invited you in for a taste in the first place.

Weizenbock

Aroma: Rich, bready malt and dark fruit.

Flavor: Sweetened wheat bread with raisins

Bitterness: 15-30 IBUs.

Strength: 6.5-8.5% abv.

Get it right and you're left with a weizenbock of complex character, soft and slamming, sweet and tart. Brewer Bill Covaleski, whose Victory Moonglow can stand aside Bavaria's best, likens it to "an alcoholic caramel apple."

Pour a glass of Schneider Aventinus, the original weizenbock invented 100 years ago, plow through the thick collar of foam, and you're rewarded with a fruit basket of aroma, a mouthful of *ohmygod*.

A lemon on this glass would be a profanity.

Weizenbock Checklist

☐ Ayinger Weizenbock (Germany)

☐ Brooklyn-Schneider Hopfen-Weisse

☐ Drei Kronen Original Schäazer Weizenbock (Germany)

☐ Eisenbahn Vigorosa (Brazil)

☐ Erdinger Pikantus (Germany)

☐ Great Lakes Glockenspiel

☐ Hacker-Pschorr Weisse Bock (Germany)

☐ Heavy Seas Hang Ten

☐ Hopf Weisser bock (Germany)

☐ Kaltenhausen Edelweiss Gamsbock (Austria)

☐ Mahrs Der Weisse Bock (Germany)

☐ Otter Creek Otterbahn.

☐ Plank Dunkler Weizenbock (Germany)

☐ Ramstein Winter Wheat

☐ Schell's Snowstorm

☐ **Schneider Aventinus** (Germany)

☐ Schneider-Brooklyner Hopfen-Weisse (Germany)

☐ Victory Moonglow

☐ Weihenstephanver Vitus (Germany)

☐ Weyerbacher Slam Dunkel

The
British Isles

Baltic Porter

For the jaded masses looking for something other than "imperial" or "double" as a description for righteous head-bangers, allow me to pitch another adjective into your lexicon: *Baltic*.

As in, "Dude, that new IPA out from California—the one with 190 IBUS and genetically enhanced hops... It's totally Baltic!"

It doesn't even have to be about beer: "Yo, check out the Baltic sound system in my basement." Or, "Did you see John Cena last night? He went Baltic on The Great Khali!"

Don't laugh. The Baltic—a European region known mainly for Russian submarine dramas and cabbage-based cuisine—is increasingly synonymous with heavy-duty porter.

How it got started, we can blame or credit the Brits. They're the ones who—apparently unable to provide the ravenous Catherine the Great with any suitable men— instead plied her with their strong (or stout) porter. They fortified the dark ale with even more alcohol to survive the freezing temps of St. Petersburg, and imperial stout was born. Naturally, not all the beer made it to Russia. Port cities in Finland, Sweden, Lithuania, Poland and elsewhere took a swallow and then added their own twist. Showing their German roots, Baltic brewers reproduced the inky porter with lager yeast that ferments at cooler temperatures.

At first glance, it's hard to tell the difference between the stout and the porter. But collect a few bottles, let them warm to about 50 degrees, and you begin to appreciate the range.

Okocim Porter from Poland, for example, comes off like a strong (8 percent alcohol), fruit-like bock. Finland's

Sinebrychoff Porter—known simply as Koff—is top-fermented like an ale, then conditioned 6 weeks at relatively warm temps. It's strong, yet smooth. Sweden's Carnegie Stark Porter is roasty and complex, but just 5.5 percent alcohol.

One of the first American Baltics was Perkuno's Hammer from the now-shuttered Heavyweight Brewing Co. in New Jersey. The beer was a collaboration between brewer Tom Baker and beer writer Lew Bryson. "The dark-fruit notes in the big Baltics Tom and I were trying to emulate come from the malt, not ale yeast," said Bryson. "They also tend to be less burnt and bitter than an imperial stout."

Bill Covaleski, whose Victory Brewing released a re-creation of the Hammer called Baltic Thunder, said, "The only important trick I see to the style is you're using a bottom-fermenting yeast on a style that was originally top fermenting beer. That creates a mellower more subdued version of porter beer."

Baltic porter

Aroma: Sweet, fruit, boozy.

Flavor:

Bitterness: 20-40 IBUs.

Strength: 5.5-10% abv.

Other craft brewers, meanwhile, have just begun to put their stamp on the style.

Southampton Publick House Imperial Porter is a strong, top-fermented porter. In Michigan, meanwhile, Shipwreck Porter is aged in used Evan Williams bourbon barrels.

The common characteristic: strength. They're totally Baltic, dude!

Baltic Porter Checklist

☐ A. Le Coq Porter (Estonia)

☐ Alaskan Baltic Porter

☐ **Aldaris Porteris** (Latvia)

☐ Arcadia Shipwreck

☐ Baltika #6 Porter (Russia)

☐ Black Boss Porter (Poland)

☐ Carnegie Porter (Sweden)

☐ Duck-Rabbit Baltic Porter

☐ Flossmoor Station Killer Kapowski

☐ Flying Dog Gonzo Imperial Porter

☐ Foothills Baltic Porer

☐ Garrison Grand Baltic Porter (Canada)

☐ Great Divide Smoked Paltic Porter

☐ Harpoon Leviathan Baltic Porter

☐ Hoogstraten Poorter (Belgium)

☐ Koutský Tmavý Speciál 18˚ (Czech)

☐ Krinitsa Porter (Belarus)

☐ Kurofune Porter (Japan)

☐ Les Trois Mousquetaires Porter Baltique (Canada)

☐ Long Trail Imperial Porter

☐ Mørke Pumpernickel Porter (Denmark)

☐ Náchod Primátor Double 24% (Czech)

☐ Okocim Porter (Poland)

☐ Ølfabrikken Porter (Denmark)

☐ Olivaria Porter (Belarus)

☐ Redoak Baltic Porter (Australia)

☐ Saku Porter (Estonia)

☐ **Sinebrychoff Porter** (Finland)

☐ Ska Nefarious Ten Pin

☐ Smuttynose Baltic Porter

☐ Southampton Imperial Baltic Porter

☐ Thisted Limfjords Porter (Denmark)

☐ Utenos Porter (Lithuania)

☐ Victory Baltic Thunder

☐ Zywiec Porter (Poland)

Braggot

A few years ago when Dogfish Head released its renowned Midas Touch Golden Elixir, I joked with brewer Sam Calagione that this unusual ale was all a terrible mistake.

His recipe was based on a high-tech analysis of residue found in 2,700-year-old goblets removed from the tomb of the historical King Midas. The testing, by molecular archeologist Patrick McGovern, showed traces of grape, honey and grain—a mixture of wine, mead and beer.

That was no special elixir they were drinking at the funeral of the ancient king, I told Calgione. Instead, surely Mrs. Midas—left to clean up the whole mess—had simply dumped everyone's dregs into a single goblet; if the scientists looked, they'd probably find cigar ashes, too.

In truth, of course, combining grain with grape or honey is no mistake. Man has toasted with this special drink for centuries.

In the case of beer mixed with mead, the drink is called braggot (or bragget or bracket or braggat or a seemingly endless variety of other spellings that have turned up through the ages). Like all matters involving the hazy history of alcohol, there is debate over its true origin.

The word seems Welsh (*brag* = malt, *got* = honeycomb, say some researchers) and, indeed, there are records of 13th-century laws that demanded freemen to pay the king of Wales enough *braccat* to fill a bathtub.

Well before that, the Irish claim, they were drinking something called *brogoit*. And no one knows how long the English celebrated Bragot Sunday, a day in which mugs of the sweet drink were raised in the midst of Lent.

What did it taste like? We can only salivate with desire when Chaucer writes in the Miller's Tale of a voluptuous, adulterous young wife whose mouth was "sweete as bragot."

At its finest, this drink would've been brewed with herbs and spices, to be served at celebrations and holy days. Ian Spencer Hornsey's *A History of Beer and Brewing* describes a medieval "up-market" version made with ginger, cinnamon, galingale and cloves.

Braggot

Aroma: Floral and honey-like.

Flavor: Balance of honey and malt, often with spice.

Bitterness: A wide range, depending on base beer style.

Strength: 5-13% abv.

More commonly, a tavern keeper would've simply mixed ale and mead—perhaps as a specialty drink, or possibly to cheat a patron who had ordered a more expensive cup of pure mead.

I've actually tried this latter method on my own, and it's not half bad—a bittersweet mingling of honey and hops. Mixing your own is certainly a lot easier than what James Taylor of Atlantic Brewing in Bar Harbor, Maine, has to go through to make his Brother Adam's Bragget Ale.

Taylor makes four 15-barrel batches over two days—each requiring 35 gallons of honey. "You ought to see the size of the squeeze bottles we use," he joked. "I never knew they made them that big!"

He spends the days cooking wort, then hoisting buckets of honey. "It's physically a busy day with lots of lifting,"

Taylor said. "It's a sticky day—you get a hell of a sugar rush just licking your fingers."

It takes more than six months of fermentation, of a gentle mingling of honey and hops. Taylor describes the finished glass as somewhere between mead and barleywine, between the kiss of honey and the bite of hops.

Even without the grapes (or cigar ashes), this braggot is worthy of a toast to a king.

Braggot Checklist

☐ Alley Kat Raspberry Mead (Canada)

☐ **Atlantic Brother Adams Bragget Ale**

☐ Bluegrass Luna De Miel Raspberry Meade

☐ Bridge Road Megachile Pluto Braggot (Australia)

☐ Crabtree Braggot

☐ Dansk Mjød Old Danish Braggot (Denmark)

☐ Kuhnhenn 9 Braggot

☐ Kuhnhenn Braggot Mead

☐ Magic Hat Braggot

☐ New Old Lompoc Bob's Memorial Braggot

☐ Purrumbete Ugly Duckling (Australia)

☐ Rabbit's Foot Bière de Miele

☐ The People's Pint Slippery Slope

☐ Thunder Head Golden Frau Honey Wheat

☐ Two Brothers Heliocentric Bragot.

☐ Viking Honey Moon

☐ Weyerbacher Sixteen

☐ White Winter Winery Brackett

☐ White Winter Winery Premium Oak Brackett

☐ Widmer Prickly Pear Braggot

☐ Želiv Castulus (Czech)

Brown Ale

Good ol' Charlie Brown. Always out there on the mound, even in the rain, ready to give his best for the rest of the "Peanuts" gang.

That's how I think of Brown Ale, the Charlie Brown of beer. It's a dependable, go-to ale; crack open a bottle of Newcastle or Turbo Dog, and you pretty much know you're going to get a malty, mildly hopped easy-drinker. Nothing over the edge. A satisfying, honest, even-tempered pal.

It's "comfort beer," said author Ray Daniels, who 10 years ago co-authored the definitive *Brown Ale: History, Brewing, Techniques, Recipes*. He notes that its toasty, biscuity, browned and caramelized flavors are also found in the foods we've been eating since man discovered fire: bread and roasted meat. "I think the flavors of kilned malt appeal to the human palate in very fundamental ways," Daniels said.

In its original English version, it is the prototypical "mild"—a light-flavored, gently hopped, low-alcohol ale intended to be drained at length. The Americans tweaked the hops and pushed the alcohol but never bastardized the style beyond recognition.

For many, Brown Ale was a gateway beer, the first time they ever dared to taste something dark. But instead of cherishing it like an old friend, some of these same beer drinkers now dismiss it as trite, almost embarrassed that they once enjoyed its simple pleasure.

You hear grumbles, for example, that Charlie Brown's a little bland, wearing that same zig-zag t-shirt every day. The west coast reaches for Lucy's bitter spirit; the old world traditionalists sing about Schroeder's classical style; the dreamers follow Snoopy's imaginative flights of fancy.

They all have a point, I suppose. Admit it, you probably wish Brown Ale was something "better"—stronger, more assertive, different. But that misses the mark on two important fronts.

If Brown Ale were maltier, it would be a porter. If it were hoppier, it would be… good grief, an Imperial Brown Ale.

More importantly, Brown Ale is no ordinary mediocrity. Take a second sip, and subtle layers of flavor and aroma unfold: the toffee of Samuel Smith's, the hazelnut of Arcadia. Look for these nuances, and the reward is fuller, more satisfying. Yet, it's not a pretentious, contemplative experience. Instead of dazzling you, the chocolate undertones of Brooklyn Brown simply invite you to pull long, long sips till you're asking for another pint. The malty wallop of Bell's Best Brown hints at a bigger beer, a cream stout perhaps, but its light body encourages you to match it with a simple burger.

> ## Brown Ale
>
> **Aroma**: Malty, light hops, fruitiness.
>
> **Flavor**:: Dark fruit, mild hops, smooth finish.
>
> **Bitterness**: 20-40 IBUs.
>
> **Strength**: 3–5% abv.
>
>

Where you once dismissed him as just a sad, conflicted soul (why isn't this dark beer more serious?), you soon find that Brown Ale is a complex individual who can hold an intelligent conversation. You just have to listen for the wonderfully nutty aside of St. George Nutty Brown, the hoppy retort of Smuttynose Old Brown Dog. Look again, and you'll find the everyday characters in the comics section are more so much more sincere than all those blowhards on the op-ed page.

Ah, you're a good man, Charlie Brown.

Brown Ale Checklist

☐ Abita Turbo Dog

☐ Ale Asylum Mad Town Nut Brown

☐ Arcadia Nut Brown

☐ Avery Ellie's Brown Ale

☐ Baird Angry Boy (Japan)

☐ Bell's Best Brown

☐ Big Sky Moose Drool

☐ Black Oak Nut Brown (Canada)

☐ Black Sheep Riggwelter Yorkshire Ale (England)

☐ Black Toad Dark Ale

☐ Brooklyn Brown Ale

☐ Carolina Cottonwood Low Down Brown

☐ Dark Horse Boffo

☐ Deschutes Buzzsaw Brown

☐ Dogfish Head Indian Brown

☐ Double Maxim Premium Brown Ale (England)

☐ Duck-Rabbit Brown Ale

☐ Flossmoor Station Pullman

☐ Half Acre Over Ale

☐ He'Brew Messiah Bold

☐ Ipswich Dark Ale

☐ Ithaca Nut Brown Ale

☐ Legend Brown Ale

☐ Lost Coast Downtown Brown

☐ Marston's Manns Brown Ale (England)

☐ Midnight Sun Kodiak Brown Ale

☐ Moose Drool Brown Ale

☐ New Glarus Fat Squirrel

☐ Newcastle Brown Ale (England)

☐ Pretty Things Saint Botolph's Town

☐ Samuel Adams Brown Ale

☐ **Samuel Smith's Nut Brown** (England)

☐ Sierra Nevada Tumbler

☐ Ska Buster Nut

☐ Smuttynose Old Brown Dog

☐ Sweetwater Georgia Brown

☐ Tommyknocker Imperial Nut Brown

☐ Troegs Rugged Trail Nut Brown

☐ Wychwood Hobgoblin (England)

India Pale Ale (English)

That English India Pale Ale is now regarded as a separate style is indictment enough of the sad state of affairs across the Atlantic.

Here is the legendary English ale, fit to be drained from a cask in a postcard London pub, intended to survive and actually improve during months at sea for export to India. The story behind this style not only recalls the creation of one of the world's great brewing capitals in Burton-on-Trent, but it harkens the triumph of the British empire, a living, breathing emblem of might and power.

India pale ale: strong, hoppy and as proud as the Union Jack.

Taxation, temperance and taste changes weakened and dulled British beer over the decades. A century after the glory, with decidedly few worthy examples brewed in the U.K., it is necessary to define English IPA as its own style—a style distinct from the modern and well-regarded variety of vigorously hopped American IPAs.

If England's George Hodgson, generally credited with "inventing" the style in the late 18th century and shipping it to India, isn't rolling over in his grave... well, fellow Brit Pete Brown certainly tossed another shovelful of dirt on his coffin with his superb book, *Hops and Glory*. Brown surveyed the English scene and—having enjoyed the likes of upstart American IPAs from Bridgeport, Dogfish Head, Goose Island and Stone breweries—declared, "The Yanks were beating us at our own game, quite embarrassingly."

British versions, like Greene King IPA, are neither hoppy nor particularly pale. "Most IPAs sold in Britain today bear scant resemblance to the ales that went to India, beyond being wet and mildly intoxicated," said Brown. At less than

4 percent alcohol by volume, they are "shadows of their former selves, just another of those arcane acronyms at the bar."

English IPAs are so pitiful, so lacking in vigor or authenticity, Brown went to the trouble of commissioning a cask of something close to the 18th century variety.

English IPA

Aroma: Moderately high hops with light, toasted malt.

Flavor: Medium-to-high hop bitterness with toffee or cookie-like malt.

Bitterness: 40-60 IBUs.

Strength: 5-7.5% abv.

Brewed at the Museum Brewery at Burton's Bass facility, Brown's ale (he called it Calcutta IPA) was made with aromatic, English-grown Northdown hops and yeast from the town's old Worthington brewery. Importantly, it was brewed with Burton's trademark water, pulled from a well at the old Salt's Brewery. Rich in gypsum, Burton water produces a sulfur nose and enhances the bitterness of ale.

A nice start.

But then—in an act of supreme and typically British eccentricity—Brown embarked on the original journey of IPA, and personally carried the damn thing by plane, train and ship from Burton to Calcutta.

The story of Brown and his cask is outstanding (you should buy the book), and it won't ruin its ending to tell you that his English IPA—the first to reach India via its traditional route in 140 years—was exactly what you'd hope for when imagining the glorious history of this style:

Hoppy up front with a caramel malt body and a smooth, dry finish.

Of course, you don't have to ship a cask thousands of miles to re-create one close to the original. Thankfully a handful of English brewers—notably Samuel Smith's and Meantime—make solid IPAs. And several Americans brew English-style IPAs, too, notching back a bit on those West Coast hops and pushing the malt forward on the palate.

But Brown's story should be required reading for all of his nation's brewers. Some day, perhaps, English IPA will once again rule the waves.

English IPA Checklist

- [ ] Alexander Keith's India Pale Ale (Canada)
- [ ] Arcadia IPA
- [ ] Belhaven Twisted Thistle (England)
- [ ] Boulder Cold Hop British-Style Ale
- [ ] Brooklyn East India Pale Ale
- [ ] Burton Bridge Empire Ale (England)
- [ ] Cricket Hill Hopnotic
- [ ] Deschutes Quail Springs
- [ ] Eel River Certified Organic IPA
- [ ] Fiddler's Green India Pale Ale
- [ ] Fuller's India Pale Ale (England)
- [ ] Goose Island India Pale Ale
- [ ] Great Lakes Commodore Perry IPA
- [ ] Harviestoun Bitter & Twisted (England)
- [ ] Left Hand 400 Pound Monkey
- [ ] Lilja's Argosy IPA
- [ ] Long Trail Traditional IPA
- [ ] Magic Hat Blind Faith
- [ ] Marston Old Empire (England)
- [ ] McEwan's India Pale Ale (Scotland)
- [ ] McNeill's Dead Horse IPA
- [ ] **Meantime India Pale Ale** (England)
- [ ] Middle Ages ImPaled Ale
- [ ] Nelson Paddywhack (Canada)
- [ ] Nils Oscar India Ale (Sweden)
- [ ] Nørrebro Bombay Pale Ale (Denmark)
- [ ] Otter Happy Otter (England)
- [ ] Propeller IPA (Canada)
- [ ] Ridgeway Bad Elf
- [ ] St. Peter's India Pale Ale
- [ ] Samuel Smith's India Ale (England)
- [ ] Shiga Kogen IPA (Japan)
- [ ] Shipyard IPA
- [ ] Short's The Golden Rule
- [ ] Spilker Hopluia
- [ ] Stazione Rajah (Italy)
- [ ] Summit India Pale Ale
- [ ] Three Floyds Blackheart
- [ ] Wells IPA (England)
- [ ] **Worthington's White Shield** (England)

Irish Red Ale

On St. Patrick's Day, you're going to hear a lot of people insist that, if you really want to be Irish for a day, you've got to drink black-as-ink stout. Either that, or green-dyed beer.

Here's another color for you to consider on this holy day of beer drinking: red, as in Irish red ale.

Hundreds of years before Arthur Guinness made his famous stout, Ireland was famous for its red ale. Poets rhapsodized about its strength and character. Believers told the tale of Conn of the Hundred Battles who, 2,000 years ago, learned the names of those who would succeed him on the throne from a beautiful, dreamlike maiden who served him ladles of ale as red as blood.

These days, unfortunately, beer freaks often skip past Irish red ale because it's faded into a style without any distinctive edges.

It is neither hoppy nor particularly malty. It is satisfying, not provocative. The official Beer Judge Certification Program style guidelines offer yawn-inducing descriptors like "moderate caramel flavor," "light grain flavor," "medium bitterness," and "easy-drinking." Another guide unhelpfully describes Irish red ale as "an Irish ale noted for its reddish color."

"It's innocuous, not super hoppy or roasty," said Kevin Reed, director of brewing operations for the Rock Bottom brewpub chain. "It's comfort beer."

At its worst, Irish-style red ale, to steal a phrase from a certain madcap celebrity, is as dull as a droopy-eyed armless child.

Jaime Jurado, director of brewing operations at the Texas-based Gambrinus Co. (Shiner beers), said that more often than not Irish red ale "may well be some brewer's imaginings of what an Irish beer should be like."

In an article he wrote for "The Brewer International" magazine, Jurado noted that the style's guidelines are so undefined that almost any amber-colored ale—from Grolsch Amber Ale to Bass—might qualify as an Irish red.

Irish red ale

Aroma: Moderate malt aroma, light buttery character, no hops.

Flavor: Some malt sweetness, buttery or toffee, low bitterness, smooth finish.

Bitterness: 15-20 IBUs.

Strength: 4-6% abv.

The difficulty of getting a handle on this variety stems mainly from widely distributed and advertised George Killian's Irish Red. Ostensibly based on the 19th-century original from Enniscorthy, Ireland, today's Killians is as ordinary as toasted Wonder Bread. No wonder: Killian's—brewed in Golden, Colo., by Coors—is neither Irish nor ale (though, for the record, it is somewhat red).

The problem is the so-called authentic originals from Ireland aren't much better.

Smithwick's, Murphy's Irish Red and Caffrey's Irish Ale all hint at malty goodness and—when served on a nitro tap—offer a creamy body. But after two or three uneventful swallows you're ready to nod off. Even O'Hara's Irish Red, from Ireland's estimable Carlow Brewing, is a watery snoozer.

Once again, it's the Americans who've taken a tired Old World style and given it new life.

Some of the domestics are classically comfortable: Brian Boru Old Irish Red from Three Floyds and Great Lakes Conway's Irish Ale are outstanding though hard to find. Easier to find is Sam Adams Irish Red, perhaps the single finest style crafted by Boston Beer. It is gentle and subtle with a solid, utterly satisfying body. It is impossible to drink a glass without saying, "Let's crack open another."

Meanwhile, other American microbrewers are jolting this subtle style with the hops equivalent of electroshock therapy. Their creation, known as Imperial Red, is super malty and overly hopped. Look especially for Lagunitas Lucky 13 Mondo Large Red Al, Terrapin Big Hoppy Monster and Flying Fish Exit 9 Hoppy Scarlet Ale, who've all pushed this style to a new and exciting dimension.

Bland? Hell no. These are red ales that are fit for Conn of Hundred Battles… or maybe even Charlie Sheen.

Irish Red Ale Checklist

- ☐ Beamish Red Ale (Ireland)
- ☐ Big Rock McNally's Extra Ale (Canada)
- ☐ Boulevard Irish Ale
- ☐ Bushwakker Dungarvon Irish Red Ale (Canada)
- ☐ Caffrey's Irish Ale (Ireland)
- ☐ Casco Bay RipTide Red Ale
- ☐ Dale Bros. Shameful McDale
- ☐ De Molen Ruig & Rood (Netherlands)
- ☐ Flying Fish Exit 9 Hoppy Scarlet Ale
- ☐ Garrison Irish Red Ale (Canada)
- ☐ Goose Island Kilgubbin Red Ale
- ☐ Harpoon Hibernian Ale
- ☐ Harviestoun Tryd & Tested (Scotland)
- ☐ Jack Russell Irish Red Ale
- ☐ Karl Strauss Red Trolley Ale
- ☐ Kilkenny Irish Cream Ale (Ireland)
- ☐ København Amarillo (Denmark)
- ☐ Lagunitas Lucky 13 Mondo Large Red Ale
- ☐ McSorley's Irish Pale Ale
- ☐ Michelob Irish Red Ale
- ☐ Moylans Dannys Irish Style Red Ale
- ☐ Murphy's Irish Red Beer (Ireland)
- ☐ Newport Storm Spring Ale
- ☐ O'Hara's Irish Red Ale (Ireland)
- ☐ Old World Irish Red Ale
- ☐ Porterhouse Red (Ireland)
- ☐ Redoak Irish Red Ale (Australia)
- ☐ Rubicon Irish Red Ale
- ☐ **Samuel Adams Irish Red**
- ☐ Saranac Irish Red Ale
- ☐ Short's The Magician
- ☐ Smithwick's Irish Ale (Ireland)
- ☐ Starr Hill Amber Ale
- ☐ Terrapin Big Hoppy Monster
- ☐ Thomas Creek River Falls Red Ale
- ☐ Thomas Hooker Irish Style Red Ale
- ☐ Three Floyds Brian Boru Old Irish Ale
- ☐ Upland Ard Ri
- ☐ Wachusett Quinn's Amber Ale
- ☐ Whitewater Clotworthy Dobbin (Ireland)

Irish Stout

Dry Irish stout tastes like Guinness, everyone knows that. The question is: What does Guinness taste like?

Over 250 years, Dublin's famous stout has evolved and morphed so many times, it's impossible to get a handle on the ale. Double Stout, Double Extra Stout, Special Export Stout, Foreign Extra Stout, Special Light Stout—Guinness has had more updates than Microsoft Windows.

Take the phenomenally popular Extra Stout, the draft whose pour they call the Perfect Pint. Smooth and roasty and dry, it's remarkably satisfying for an ale that barely tips the scales at about 4 percent alcohol. It's so low in calories, its owner, Diageo, once issued press releases bragging that, ounce for ounce, Guinness Stout has fewer calories than skimmed milk. Yet, in the mid-19th century, this very same brand—the one would eventually epitomize dear, quaffable, session-like Irish stout—buoyed the hydrometer to 1.074 original gravity. Don't bother pulling out your calculator; that's barleywine territory. Which is to say, if the original Irish stout were to be submitted to an Irish stout judging panel, it would end up in the dump bucket with the rest of the losers.

The changing nature of Guinness, and thus this style, shouldn't be a surprise because, says author Bill Yenne, the original Irish stout itself was the product of evolution.

"Arthur Guinness didn't create the style," said Yenne, who chronicled the brewery's history in *Guinness: The 250-Year Quest for the Perfect Pint*. "You've got to remember, brewers were making it up as they went along. The style has a family tree with many branches, and they all go way back before Guinness."

If anything, it begins with porter, the dark ale attributed to English brewer Ralph Harwood, circa 1722. As with India pale ale, porter brewers made stiffer export versions—more alcohol, more hops—to survive the long journey to the colonies. In the 1820s, Guinness would begin brewing Extra Superior Porter—a stronger porter, a *stout* porter. "Stout was an adjective," said Yenne. "It was a porter, but more so."

Irish stout

Aroma: Roasted barley and coffee with very low hops.

Flavor: Bitter roasted grain with bittersweet chocolate and light sourness. Creamy body.

Bitterness: 3-45 IBUs.

Strength: 4-5% abv.

What did that beer taste like? It was probably something like today's hard-to-find Guinness Foreign Export Stout, said Yenne: rich and strong (7% abv) and bittersweet, a far cry from what these days we call an Irish stout.

Changes in ingredients and strength are not unheard of as styles evolve. What came to typify modern Irish stout, however, was more likely the change in bubbles.

In 1959, Guinness discovered that the secret to a long-lasting, mustache-producing head of foam was nitrogen. Nitrogen, mixed with CO_2, gave the stout a creamier mouthfeel, a lively, surprisingly thirst-quenching body that allowed pub sitters to drain pint after pint.

It's this draft Guinness Extra Stout—cascading with bubbles often topped with the imprint of a shamrock—that comes to mind when we think of Irish stout: dark with the burnt-toast bitterness of roasted malt, dry with a touch of unmalted barley, creamy with flaked barley, complex with a touch of soured ale. It sucks down like an adult milkshake, each gulp leaving behind a telltale ring of clinging foam.

There are others, of course, notably Beamish and Murphy's. But few outside of Cork think of either when asked to name an Irish Stout.

"Guinness defines the style," Yenne said. "because Guinness dominates the category."

Irish Stout Checklist

- ☐ Anheuser-Busch Bare Knuckle Stout
- ☐ Avery Out of Bounds
- ☐ Baden Baden Dark Ale Stout (Brazil)
- ☐ Baird Shimaguni Stout (Japan)
- ☐ Beamish Stout (Ireland)
- ☐ Cavalry Nomad's Stout
- ☐ Christian Moerlein Friend Of An Irishman
- ☐ Dark Starr Stout
- ☐ De La Senne Stouterik (Belgium)
- ☐ Del Ducato Sally Brown (Italy)
- ☐ Dungarvan Black Rock (Ireland)
- ☐ Furthermore Three Feet Deep
- ☐ Golden Lion Stout (Canada)
- ☐ Gritty McDuff's Black Fly
- ☐ Guinness Draft (Ireland)
- ☐ **Guinness Extra Stout** (Ireland)
- ☐ Hockley Valley Stout (Canada)
- ☐ Lakefront Snake Chaser
- ☐ Le Naufrageur Saint-Barnabé (Canada)
- ☐ Minerva Stout (Mexico)
- ☐ Moylans Dragoons Dry Irish Stout
- ☐ Murphy's Irish Stout (Ireland)
- ☐ North Coast Black Hart
- ☐ North Coast Old No. 38
- ☐ Nynäshamns Sotholmen Stout (Sweden)
- ☐ O'Hara's Irish Stout (Ireland)
- ☐ Old Nutfield Black 47
- ☐ Trio Extra Stout (Netherlands)
- ☐ Paper City Riley's Stout
- ☐ Porterhouse Oyster Stout (Ireland)
- ☐ Porterhouse Wrasslers 4X Stout (Ireland)
- ☐ Portsmouth Black Cat Stout
- ☐ Saranac Irish Stout
- ☐ Shipyard Blue Fin
- ☐ Short's Uncle Steve's Irish Stout
- ☐ **Sly Fox O'Reilly's Irish Stout**
- ☐ Sprecher Irish Style Stout
- ☐ Three Floyd's Black Sun Stout
- ☐ Victory Donnybrook

Mild Ale

Mild needs an aggressive public relations campaign, an image consultant, maybe even a personal trainer. Otherwise, one of the world's most misunderstood beer styles will never shed its reputation for mediocrity.

Robust, virile, full of character—these are the virtues we admire in our favorite beer.

Mild? Just take a look at some of the lifeless adjectives the style mavens use to describe our hero: "moderate," "medium," "ordinary," and perhaps the worst, "session"—as if one might enjoy this ale only under the wearisome circumstances we usually associate with time spent on a psychiatrist's couch.

Oh, yes, you can drink a Mild all night. Big deal. Here's what else you can do all night: Snore.

See how easy it is to shrug off poor Mild? You might as well call it Bland and stack it on the shelf next to Wonder Bread.

In fact, as anyone with an appreciation for the sublime can testify, a well-brewed Mild is anything but lifeless. Served from a cask, it fills the mouth with light wisps of malty goodness, ranging from delicate caramel to toasted bread. Each quaff of Mild is as refreshing as the last, never bitter, always low enough in alcohol (under 4% abv) to maintain a passably sober equilibrium.

Curiously, Mild's name originally had nothing to do with its buzz capacity.

It got its name to distinguish it from aged beer, like porter. "It meant that the drink was still young and hadn't acquired the tarter, sourer characteristics that aged beers developed…" said author Martyn Cornell, who has written extensively about British beer styles.

But mild-mannered? Not at all. In the early 19th century, it wouldn't be unusual to find a Mild clocking in at 7 or 8 percent alcohol by volume, Cornell said.

All beer evolves, naturally. Grain shortages during World War I and British tax laws conspired to reduce the original gravity, and thus the alcohol.

Mild Ale

Aroma: Moderate malt, nuttiness or caramel.

Flavor: Delicate but complex malt flavors, including fruit, caramel, toffee, chocolate, molasses.

Bitterness: 10-25 IBUs.

Strength: 2.8—4% abv.

Its popularity weakened as tastes changed. "Mild was what you drank in the rougher public bar," Cornell said. "Bitter was in the more up-market saloon bar." By the 1960s, young drinkers turned their back on Your Father's Beer, and mild all but disappeared.

Today, only a handful of traditional cask beer brewers still make it in England. A few American brewers have taken a stab at it, however.

One of them—Yards Brewing of Philadelphia— brews a British-style Dark Mild in bottles and draft. I asked its brewer, Tom Kehoe, what he was shooting for in the new beer.

"I always go back to Batemans XB, which is one of my absolute favorite beers," said Kehoe. "It's just a style that has a really nice malt character. It just rolls down your throat."

His beer is smooth and malty and, yeah, you can pound it all night. But can Mild finally shed its mild image?

Yards sounds like they hired that personal trainer. Its Mild is called Brawler, a "Pugilist-Style Ale."

Mild Ale Checklist

This style is vastly improved when pulled from a cask

- ☐ Adnam's Bitter (England)
- ☐ Alexander Keith's Dark Ale (Canada)
- ☐ Bank Top Dark Mild (England)
- ☐ Bar Harbor Lighthouse Ale
- ☐ **Bateman's XB** (England)
- ☐ Belhaven Best (England)
- ☐ Brakspear Bitter (England)
- ☐ Cains Dark Mild (England)
- ☐ Coopers Dark Ale (Australia)
- ☐ F&M Stonehammer Dark Ale (Canada)
- ☐ Fuller's Chiswick Bitter (England)
- ☐ Gale's Festival Mild (England)
- ☐ Grand River Mill Race Mild (Canada)
- ☐ Iceni Men of Norfolk (England)
- ☐ Leeds Midnight Bell (England)
- ☐ Listermann Wild Mild
- ☐ London Ruby Anglaise (Canada)
- ☐ Moorhouse Black Cat (England)
- ☐ **Original Sarah Hughes Dark Ruby Mild** (England)
- ☐ Revelation Cat Milk Mild (Italy)
- ☐ Snipes Mountain Coyote Moon
- ☐ Surly Mild
- ☐ Theakston Traditional Mild (England)
- ☐ Three Floyds Pride & Joy
- ☐ Tooheys Old (Australia)
- ☐ Whistler Original Black Tusk Ale (Canada)
- ☐ Yards Brawler

Milk/Sweet Stout

You've gotta love the scientific mind, circa 1877:

An author identified in the French *Journal d' Hygiene* as A. Chevallier opined that, if beer is good for you, and milk is good for you, then beer made with milk instead of water has to be even better. His imagined concoction, *La Biere de Lait*, would combine the restorative qualities of malt and hops with the nutritional components of milk.

With rock solid logic like that, it's a wonder, in our modern century, we don't drink beer through straws from cartons labeled with pictures of missing kids.

Alas, no one ever devised a palatable milk beer, possibly because it's a lot easier to turn a tap than yank an udder. But they came pretty close with milk stout.

Creamy and wholesome and chocolatey as that glass of Nesquik you used to dunk your Oreos into, milk stout—a.k.a. cream stout or sweet stout—seemingly comes straight from the dairy. Yet, it contains not an ounce of moo-juice.

The story behind its name goes back even before those grand days of 19th-century milk and beer experimentation.

It stems from the age-old practice of adding sugar to beer, to create a festive punch, or to take the edge off of overly tart or sour beer. Ancient texts speak of sweetening beer with honey or nectar. In an 1869 treatise, *Cups and their Customs,* there is a description of the "Freemasons Cup," which consisted of a pint of Scotch ale, a pint of mild, a half pint of brandy, a pint of sherry and *a half-pound of sugar.* The practice lives even today, in the small children who stir teaspoons of sugar into their low-alcohol faro at Brussels' famed Café Mort Subite.

Sugar, however, had another benefit: added calories. The medical literature of the 19th century is filled with advice to feed sweetened beer—especially dark and rich stout—to the pale and sickly. Whether the patient had tuberculosis or was simply pregnant, those extra pounds couldn't hurt; if nothing else, the booze certainly dulled the pain.

From that standpoint, A. Chevallier hardly sounds like a crackpot. Indeed, it was only a matter of time till someone wondered: If brewing beer with milk is out of the question, what if you simply added the *essence* of milk?

The essence, these deep-thinkers suggested, is lactose—milk sugar.

By the end of the century, several competing scientists had filed for patents for some type of lactose-spiked beer. The idea leaped from theory to practice in 1907, when the Mackeson brewery in England bottled the first milk stout, labeled with an old-fashioned creamery churn.

Milk/Sweet Stout

Aroma: Mild roasted grain with chocolate notes.

Flavor: Rich, dark malt with a creamy smooth, sometimes dominate sweetness.

Bitterness: 20-40 IBUs.

Strength: 4-6% abv.

"Each pint," Mackeson slickly claimed, "contains the energising carbohydrates of ten ounces of pure dairy milk."

One hundred years later, the curative value of sweetened beer has been mostly debunked; we know that lactose contains none of the important fats or proteins (the true essence) of milk, and carbs are a dirty word.

But that doesn't make milk stout any less a marvel. Lactose will not ferment with typical beer yeast, so its latent sweetness balances the dark ale's roasted malts, typically with a creamy body. Other similar sweet stouts achieve the same quality with sucrose. Even if it isn't quite *La Biere de Lait,* surely a pint of richly complex Duck-Rabbit Milk Stout from North Carolina or lusciously creamy Lancaster Milk Stout from Pennsylvania is exactly what the doctor ordered.

Milk/Sweet Stout Checklist

- ☐ Banks Milk Stout (Guyana)
- ☐ Bell's Special Double Cream Stout
- ☐ Brau Brothers Moo Joos Oatmeal Milk Stout
- ☐ Butternuts Moo Thunder Stout
- ☐ Carib Royal Extra Stout (Trinidad & Tobago)
- ☐ Carlton & United Sheaf Stout (Australia)
- ☐ Castle Milk Stout (South Africa)
- ☐ Cerveza Jerome Negra (Argentina)
- ☐ Charlevoix Vache Folle Imperial Milk Stout (Canada)
- ☐ Dark Horse Too Cream Stout.
- ☐ **Duck-Rabbit Milk Stout**
- ☐ Farsons Lacto Traditional Stout Beer (Malta)
- ☐ Hitachino Nest Sweet Stout (Japan)
- ☐ Horny Goat Stacked Milk Stout
- ☐ Keegan Mothers Milk Stout
- ☐ Lancaster Cream Stout
- ☐ Left Hand Milk Stout
- ☐ Mackeson's XXX Stout (England)
- ☐ Mogollon Apache Trout
- ☐ Nørrebro La Granja Stout (Denmark)
- ☐ O'Fallon Chocolate by the Barrel
- ☐ Portsmouth Milk Stout
- ☐ River Horse Oatmeal Milk Stout
- ☐ St. Peter's Cream Stout (England)
- ☐ Samuel Adams Cream Stout
- ☐ Ska Steel Toe Stout
- ☐ South Shore Rhoades Scholar Stout
- ☐ Staropramen Kelt (Czech)
- ☐ Tallgrass Buffalo Sweat
- ☐ Tennent's Sweetheart Stout (England)
- ☐ Terrapin Moo-Hoo Chocolate Milk Stout
- ☐ Three Floyds Moloko
- ☐ Trois Dames La Semeuse Espresso Stout (Switzerland)
- ☐ Twisted Pine Cream Style
- ☐ Van Steenberge Wilson Mild Stout (Belgium)
- ☐ Williamsburg AleWerks Coffeehouse Stout

Oatmeal Stout

Eat your oatmeal!

At 8 years of age and with a sour attitude about putting a spoonful of gloopy, gray, gelatinous gunk to my mouth, I never imagined there'd be a day I might actually like the stuff. And I'm not talking about the barely edible bowlfuls I choke down these mornings upon advice and arm-twisting from the appetite terminators at the American Medical Association.

When it comes to enhancing the flavor of oatmeal, the only real solution is a half cup of brown sugar.

Or a glass of Samuel Smith's Oatmeal Stout. Dark and handsome with a brown collar of foam, this is a deliciously filling beer that seems, well, wholesome. Knock back a couple of them and you can almost feel your cholesterol dropping.

Indeed, a century ago that was the main selling point of oatmeal stout. Years before advertisers told us that "Guinness is good for you," doctors and midwives were prescribing regular pints of oatmeal stout for a variety of ailments. The Chamberlain & Smith beer importers of Norwich, England, advertised in 1908 that its oatmeal stout was "most invigorating for athletes." Mothers were told to drink a glass at noontime to promote breast milk production—an old wives tale that the Journal of American Medicine was unable to debunk as late as 1913.

Wartime ingredient shortages doomed the beer; by the 1930s there wasn't a single English brewery that made the glorious stout. It was extinct for 50 years, till beer importer Charlie Finkel persuaded Samuel Smith's to give it go. Today, there are at least 300 different varieties, including outstanding versions from Anderson Valley, McAuslan and Breckinridge. Wolaver's makes an organic oatmeal stout, Stoudt's Fat Dog is an imperial (9 percent alcohol) oatmeal.

Well made, oatmeal stout is a rich, satisfying ale that invites you to pull one pint after another. Up front, it greets your tongue with a slight burnt edge; rather than rudely overwhelming your palate, though, the bitterness quickly smoothes out with silky tides of roasty malt flavor and a sweet finish.

Yum, you might finally concede, oatmeal sure tastes good.

Not so fast. The oatmeal in that brew doesn't provide much flavor. In fact, oatmeal stout typically contains only 5 to 10 percent oatmeal; any more, and the brewer faces a big, pasty mess that makes it exceptionally hard to properly lauter the batch. That roasted flavor comes from the same malt you'd find in any other stout. You probably notice the sweetness because it contains fewer hops.

"Oatmeal isn't really a flavor," said Patrick Jones, former brewer at Triumph Brewing in Philadelphia. "It's a texture." The oatmeal, he said, mainly provides proteins that have a molecular structure that gives the beer that velvety smooth feel in your mouth. Many breweries enhance that sensation by serving it on nitrogen taps, like the ones that pour Guinness.

Oatmeal Stout

Aroma: Roasted, coffee-like with low hops.

Flavor: Lightly sweet with complex roasted grains.

Bitterness: 25-40 IBUs.

Strength: 4.5—6% abv.

But place, say, an Alaskan Stout side by side with a Guinness, and you might never go back to Ireland. Creamy, dark and mellow, it slays you with a complex array of flavor: chocolate, caramel, coffee.

Your morning bowl of oatmeal never tasted so good.

Oatmeal Stout Checklist

□ Alaskan Stout

□ Alley Kat Three Bears (Canada)

□ **Anderson Valley Barney Flats**

□ Angry Minnow Oakys Oatmeal Stout

□ Arcadia Starboard Stout

□ Belfast Bay McGovern's Oatmeal Stout

□ Breckenridge Oatmeal Stout

□ Broughton Scottish Oatmeal Stout (Scotland)

□ Dark Horse One

□ El Toro Negro Oatmeal Stout

□ Elysian Dragon's Tooth Oatmeal Stout

□ Erie Drake's Crude

□ Firestone Walker Velvet Merlin

□ Goose Island Oatmela Stout

□ Lost Coast 8 Ball Stout

□ McAuslan St. Ambroise (Canada)

□ Mercury Ipswitch

□ Mikkeller Beer Geek Breakfast (Denmark)

□ New Glarus Road Slush

□ New Holland The Poet

□ Nimbus Oatmeal Stout

□ Ninkasi Oatis

□ **Rogue Shakespeare Stout**

□ Samuel Smith's Oatmeal Stout (England)

□ Sand Creek Oscar's Chocolate Oatmeal Stout

□ Troegs Java Head Stout

□ Wolaver's Oatmeal Stout

□ Young's Oatmeal Stout

Oyster Stout

"He was a bold man," wrote 18th-century Irish satirist Jonathan Swift, "that first eat an oyster." But no less bold was the first brewer who added oysters to his stout. After all, salty, squishy and arousing are not adjectives one normally associates with beer.

And, yet, lately we're seeing a unexpected surge in the quirky style known as oyster stout:

- Harpoon Brewing produced Island Creek Oyster Stout, made with freshly harvested Massachusetts oysters.
- Upright Brewing bottled a limited-edition batch of its Oyster Stout, made with 30 pounds of oysters and oyster liquor.
- The 2011 Craft Brewers Conference in San Francisco featured a symposium beer from California's Iron Springs, Marin and Magnolia breweries, made with 1,000 local oysters.

The unusual variety is not about to supplant the likes of Guinness or even cultish Russian imperial stout. But the growing popularity of oyster stout surely takes the whole food-and-beer pairing trend to another level.

Indeed, that's where the entire idea of dumping bivalves into the kettle began: Beer-drinkers have always known that the roastiness of strong, cold, dark beer was the perfect complement to a briny oyster.

In *Beer & Food: An American History*, author Bob Skilnik writes, "It's always amusing to read about the contemporary beer writer or cookbook author who 'discovers' the tastiness of pairing something like a stout with a chilled oyster, when Dutch patroons were already sluppering down beers and oysters at places like the White Horse Tavern more than 350 years earlier."

By the 1850s, so-called Oyster Saloons were as common in big cities as McDonald's are today. A Scottish writer named Charles Mackay (a latter-day de Tocqueville) marveled at the "Oyster and Lager Beer Saloons" of New York City's Broadway, where "oysters as large as a lady's hand are to be had at all hours." In Philadelphia, he wrote, "The rich consume oysters and Champagne; the poorer classes consume oysters and lager bier…"

But actually brewing beer with oysters?

Michael Jackson traced that brave idea to New Zealand, where in 1929 the Young & Son Portsmouth Brewery produced Victory Oyster Stout. British breweries would take up the practice as part of the trend of supplementing stout with nutrients (milk, sugar, etc.) for added nourishment.

The health benefits are dubious. Meanwhile, the brewers I've spoken to offer mixed assessments on the impact of oysterized brews.

Oyster Stout

Aroma: Roasted grain, some fruitiness, hint of salt

Flavor: Dark grains, some coffe notes, dry finish

Bitterness: 20-60 IBUs.

Strength: 4-7% abv.

It's said that the calcium in the shells helps clarify the beer and enhance body. Others think the shellfish reduce acidity, which will help produce a better head. When Cherry Hill's Flying Fish Brewing released its one-off Exit

1 Bayshore Oyster Stout, the company said the oysters improved its dryness.

The oyster meat itself mostly dissolves during the brewing process, and it takes a refined palate to detect even a hint of saltiness.

Perhaps most importantly, adding oysters underscores what is truly one of the great bar food delights of all time. My own heaven is an ivory-handed shucker delicately icing endless plates of fresh Quonset Points while I sit on a stool, watching and sluppering from a bottomless pint of black-as-ink Irish stout. The bite of Tabasco is a temptation; the brine and vinegar are a seduction; the roasted malt is a mouthy kiss.

No question, oysters are an aphrodisiac.

Oyster Stout Checklist

□ Adnams Oyser Stout (England)

□ Bushy's Oyster Stout (Isle of Man)

□ Gadds Black Pearl Oyster Stout (England)*

□ Harpoon Island Creek Oyster Stout

□ Iwate Kura Oyster Stout (Japan)

□ **Marston's Oyster Stout (England)***

□ Porterhouse Oyster Stout (England)

□ Rogue Oyster Cloyster Stout?

□ Three Boys Oyster Stout (New Zealand)

□ Upright Oyster Stout

□ Whitstable Oyster Stout (England)

□ **Yards Love Stout**

*Not brewed with oysters.

Russian Imperial Stout

W here would lovers of the world's strongest, darkest beers be without a thin, pale German teen-ager named Sophia Augusta Frederica?

One of the great chapters of brewing history might not exist. There'd be no stouts named Old Rasputin or The Czar or Ivan the Terrible. On the upside, the tiresome debate over whether to call it "double" or "imperial" IPA would never have started.

Indeed, no fewer than one-third of Beer Advocate.com's top 100 beers would be classified as something pedestrian (Estonian Extra Porter, maybe?) if sickly, 16-year-old Sophia hadn't been dragged off to St. Petersburg in 1745 by her throne-chasing mother to marry her second cousin and become, as your 10th-grade history teacher surely taught you, Catherine II, the Empress of all the Russias.

Catherine the Great (according to the oft-repeated legend) had a passion for the brownest, strongest porter from London's great Anchor brewery. It was this ale that would eventually evolve into possibly the grandest of all beer styles, the darling of extreme beer aficionados, the prototype for some of the world's most treasured brands: Russian Imperial Stout.

There's no definitive source on how the empress discovered the dark ale. Perhaps it was during a visit to England, or maybe as she enjoyed its restorative powers during a spell with pneumonia. I have another theory:

The monarch's chamberlain — or chief of staff—was a brilliant Russian count named Andrei Shuvalov. It was Shuvalov who likely wrote most of Catherine's letters, and it was Shuvalov who spread many of those nasty rumors about her notorious sexual peccadilloes (though probably not the one about the horse). The count was also a good friend of the famous British diarist James Boswell, the friend and biographer of one Dr. Samuel Johnson.

Johnson was close friends with the owner of the Anchor Brewery, a member of Parliament named Henry Thrale; in fact, Johnson actually lived on and off in a room at the brewery along the bank of the Thames at Southwark. At the time, Anchor was well known for its exceptionally strong version of porter which had been exported to the Balkans.

It's not a hard stretch to imagine that Catherine the Great learned of this beer from her chamberlain, who might have been introduced to it by Boswell. In any case, we do know that the empress's royal court ordered enough shipments of the strong porter that it would become known as *Imperial* Brown Stout.

When Thrale died in 1781, it was Johnson who—as estate executioner—uttered one the beer world's most enduring quotes: "We are not here to sell a parcel of boilers and vats, but the potentiality of growing rich beyond the dreams of avarice." His prediction came true as the new owners, John Perkins and David Barclay, would turn Anchor into the largest brewery in the world before it was acquired by John Courage.

Russian Imperial Stout

Aroma: Roasted grain, hops, alcohol with coffee or chocolate notes.

Flavor: Strong, complex maltiness, bittersweet with slight burnt grain, low carbonation.

Bitterness: 50-90 IBU's.

Strength: 8-12% abv.

It is the version of Russian Imperial Stout brewed by Courage that old-timers still talk about. Roasty, aromatic, almost fruity and quite strong (10 percent alcohol by volume), this stout surely warmed more than a few Russian souls over the centuries. Sadly extinct since the '90s, it has been ably replaced by dozens of English and American varieties—all of whom owe a debt to dear Sophia Augusta Frederica.

Russian Imperial Stout Checklist

- ☐ AleSmith Speedway Stout
- ☐ Avery the Czar
- ☐ Bell's Expedition
- ☐ **Brooklyn Black Chocolate Stout**
- ☐ Brooklyn Black Ops
- ☐ Cigar City Marshal Zhukov's Imperial Stout
- ☐ Dark Horse Plead the 5th
- ☐ De Struise Black Albert (Belgium)
- ☐ Deschutes the Abyss
- ☐ Duck-Rabbit Rabid Duck
- ☐ Ellezelloise Hercule (Belgium)
- ☐ Foothills Sexual Chocolate
- ☐ Founders Imperial Stout
- ☐ Founders Kentucky Breakfast Stout
- ☐ Goose Island Bourbon County Stout
- ☐ Great Divide Yeti
- ☐ Great Lakes Blackout Stout
- ☐ HaandBryggeriet Dark Force (Norway)
- ☐ Heavy Seas Peg Leg
- ☐ Hoppin' Frog B.O.R.I.S. the Crusher
- ☐ **Le Coq Imperial Extra Double Stout** (England)
- ☐ Left Hand Imperial Stout
- ☐ Leinenkugel Big Eddy
- ☐ Middle Ages Dragonslayer
- ☐ Mikkeller Black Hole (Denmark)
- ☐ Moylan's Ryan Sullivan's Imperial Stout
- ☐ New England Imperial Storm Trooper
- ☐ Nøgne Ø Dark Horizon (Norway)
- ☐ North Coast Old Rasputin
- ☐ Oskar Blues Ten Fidy
- ☐ Port Brewing Santa's Little Helper
- ☐ Portsmouth Kate the Great
- ☐ Samuel Smith's Imperial Stout (England)
- ☐ Smuttynose Imperial Stout
- ☐ Stone Imperial Stout
- ☐ Surly Darkness
- ☐ Thirsty Dog Siberian Night
- ☐ Three Floyds Dark Lord
- ☐ Victory Storm King
- ☐ Weyerbacher Heresy

Scotch Ale

When in Scotland, don't ask what's in the haggis, don't ask what's underneath the kilt, and for god's sake don't ask for a Scotch ale.

You're going to get a strange look from the bartender and then... who knows? He might pour you anything from Belhaven 60 Shilling, which at 3 percent alcohol is light-bodied and amber, to Dark Island, which at 10 percent alcohol will have you thinking barleywine.

Scotch ale in Scotland? It's like asking for a quarter-pounder in France.

It's only when you the leave the country that Scotch ale is singularly defined as a comfortably numbing, strong, dark malt bomb. McEwan's, Orkney, Traquair House, MacAndrew's —these are the rich, malty brews that we're after when we order a Scotch ale, a bracing sip for the cold months ahead. It'll have you pulling on a tartan sweater and quoting Robbie Burns:

> *The night drave on wi' sangs an' clatter;*
> *And aye the ale was growing better.*

Strong enough to shake off the chills of a misty bog—that is Scotch ale.

The country's other, lighter beers are carefully (if not ridiculously) distinguished as *"Scottish"* ale. More precisely, those ales—malty but less filling—are labeled as 60-, 70-, and 80-shilling ales, denoting the strength and the price one paid long ago.

But it is the strong, hearty Scotch ale that we're thirsting for here, what has become known, no less confusingly, as Wee Heavy. (The name originates from a heavy beer once made by the old Fowler's brewery outside of Edinburgh and served in a wee bottle.)

Poured into a thistle glass, a classic Scotch ale's malt aroma rises in an earthy, perhaps smoky haze of sweetness. It possesses a clean, caramel character, the product of a long, cool fermentation and the near-absence of hops. The alcohol might climb to 8 percent or more, but you won't notice till the warmth reaches your toes.

This is the flavor and character that American craft brewers like Founders, Arcadia and Sam Adams had in mind when they brewed their own versions of Scotch ale.

It's no misplaced stereotype, either, for this is the style that Scotland chose to export to the rest of the world so long ago.

After World War I, it was McEwan's heavy ale that found its way to Belgium, creating a loyal fan base that lives today. (Did you know, by the way, that Duvel— Belgium's outstanding strong golden ale— purportedly took its original yeast from a bottle of McEwan's?)

> **Scotch Ale**
>
> **Aroma**: Malt, caramel, no hops.
>
> **Flavor**: Rich with roasted malt and sweet caramel.
>
> **Bitterness**: 17-35 IBUs.
>
> **Strength**: 6-10% abv.
>
>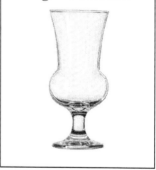

Before that, it was strong, dark Scottish ales that Londoners savored as a medicinal bracer. In a memorable passage from a medical journal in the 1850s, a physician reported one of his patients survived for 15 years on nothing more than a daily teaspoon of cod's liver oil and this beloved ale. The doctor reported, "…He slept well, and suffered but comparatively little."

Surely, the great 19th-century French chef and food historian Alexis Soyer had enjoyed a glass or three when he wrote, "Scotch ale is a seductive drink, and as perfidious as pleasure: it bewilders the senses and finally masters the reason."

Seductive and perfidious. The same goes for haggis… and kilts.

Scotch Ale Checklist

- ☐ AleSmith Wee Heavy
- ☐ Antares Scotch (Argentina)
- ☐ Arcadia Loch Down
- ☐ Belhaven Wee Heavy (Scotland)
- ☐ Berkshire Gude Greg's
- ☐ Bridgeport Highland Ambush
- ☐ Broughton Old Jock (Scotland)
- ☐ Dark Horse Scotty Karate
- ☐ Du Ciel Équinoxe Du Printemps (Canada)
- ☐ Duck-Rabbit Wee Heavy
- ☐ Erie Ol' Red Cease and Desist
- ☐ Founders Backwoods Bastard
- ☐ Founders Dirty Bastard
- ☐ Grand Teton Sheep Eater
- ☐ Great Divide Claymore
- ☐ Kettlehouse Cold Smoke
- ☐ L'abri De La Tempête Corne De Brume (Canada)
- ☐ Le Bilboquet MacKroken Flower (Canada)
- ☐ MacAndrew's Scotch Ale (Scotland)
- ☐ **McEwan's Scotch Ale (Scotland)**
- ☐ Moylan's Kilt Lifter
- ☐ Orkney Skull Splitter (Scotland)
- ☐ **Oskar Blues Old Chub**
- ☐ Pike Kilt Lifter
- ☐ Red Hill Scotch Ale (Australia)
- ☐ Renaissance Stonecutter (New Zealand)
- ☐ Samuel Adams Scotch Ale
- ☐ Schlafly Scotch Style
- ☐ Scotch Silly (Belgium)
- ☐ Smuttynose Scotch Style Ale
- ☐ Sprecher Pipers
- ☐ Stone Highway 78
- ☐ Summit 90
- ☐ Terrapin 90 Shelling
- ☐ Traquair House Ale (Scotland)
- ☐ **Traquair Jacobite (Scotland)**

Winter Warmer

Who in the name of Reinheitsgebot thought it was a good idea to dump spices— nutmeg, cinnamon, vanilla—into beer? Every winter it's the same thing: Brewers around the world (despite seasonal admonitions to bring good will toward all men) nevertheless tear open the pantry cabinet and pour bucketfuls of powders, flowers, fruits and secret potions into perfectly good vats of beer.

These are supposed to be alcoholic beverages for adults, not gingerbread cookies for runny-nosed urchins.

Bah humbug!

Ah… don't listen to me. That's just my inner Scrooge.

In fact, spiced holiday brews—call them winter warmers or Christmas beers, depending on your secularity—have a long, flavorful history that undoubtedly pre-dates the Bavarian beer purity law. Rather than a perversion, spiced ale is the original beer.

And by original, I mean not quite dawn of man, but back to a time when the changing of seasons was a cause for pagan celebration. In the case of winter, it was the time of Saturnalia in Rome, Yule in Scandinavia—huge, weeklong feasts to mark the death and rebirth of the sun and the earth.

As you might imagine, there was a bit of drinking that went on.

Those early beers were bittered not necessarily with hops, but with a combination of herbs and spices—heather, juniper, yarrow, coriander, anise. The spices balanced the sweet malt, preserved the beer and, if you listen to Wiccans, held mystical healing powers. Since everybody was in a celebratory mood, brewers would've made something special, perhaps spicier or more potent.

The rest of the story you know: Rheinheitsgebot declared spices verbotten in favor of hops, Prohibition killed American brewing tradition and big brewers dumbed down everything they touched. All hope was lost till Fritz Maytag descended from the heavens, saved San Francisco's Anchor Brewing and, in 1975, re-introduced Christmas beer to the faithful.

It wasn't till about 10 years later that Anchor actually started adding spices to Our Special Ale, but by then it was anything goes. Pagans at heart, craft brewers across the land began turning out their own special ales to mark the winter solstice.

Sweetwater Festive from Georgia has the flavor of cinnamon and mace. Sly Fox from Pennsylvania is mulled with ginger and nutmeg. Hitachino Nest Celebration from Japan is flavored with orange peel and vanilla beans.

Winter Warmer

Aroma: Sweet, spicy.

Flavor: Malty, dried fruit, nutty, spiced.

Bitterness: Varies.

Strength: 6-10% abv.

It can be tough, though, to make your way through an entire case of those flavors; some are as intense as a cup of Red Zinger tea. Unopened bottles might sit 'til July in the back of the fridge, along with your Aunt Irma's fruitcake.

Thus, some winter warmers—Samuel Smith's and Young's, as prime examples—have no spices at all. Their malty character evokes the flavor of a warm cup of wassail.

Others, like Samuel Adams Old Fezziwig, are so mild, the spices seem intended to enhance the finish of the hops rather than tickle your tongue.

In any case, there's usually an underlying sweet, malty base to winter warmers—something like an English old ale. The alcohol takes the chill off, the hops are just dry enough to make you want another... and another.

Just like a fresh-baked gingerbread cookie.

Winter Warmer Checklist

- ☐ 21st Amendment Fireside Chat
- ☐ Alaskan Winter Ale
- ☐ **Anchor Our Special Ale**
- ☐ Anderson Valley Winter Solstice
- ☐ Boulder Never summer
- ☐ Breckenridge Christmas
- ☐ BridgePort Ebenezer
- ☐ Carolina Cottonwood Frostbite
- ☐ Deschutes Jubelale
- ☐ Dundee Festive Ale
- ☐ Flying Dog K-9 Cruiser
- ☐ Full Sail Wassail
- ☐ Fuller's Old Winter Ale (England)
- ☐ Goose Island Christmas Ale
- ☐ Great Lakes Christmas Ale
- ☐ Harpoon Winter Warmer
- ☐ Harveys Christmas Ale (England)
- ☐ Highgate Old Ale (England)
- ☐ J.W. Lees Moonraker (England)
- ☐ Jamtlands Julöl (Sweden)
- ☐ Lakefront Holiday Spice Lager Beer
- ☐ Nils Oscar Julöl (Sweden)
- ☐ North Coast Wintertime Ale
- ☐ Odell Isolation
- ☐ Pike Auld Acquaintance
- ☐ Pyramid Snow Cap
- ☐ Samuel Adams Old Fezziwig (England)
- ☐ Samuel Adams Winter Lager
- ☐ **Samuel Smith's Winter Welcome (England)**
- ☐ Shipyard Prelude
- ☐ Sly Fox Christmas Ale
- ☐ Stevens Point St. Benedict's Winter Ale
- ☐ Sweetwater Festive Ale
- ☐ Wellington Iron Duke (Canada)
- ☐ Weyerbacher Winter ale
- ☐ Widmer Brrr
- ☐ Wychwood Bah Humbug (England)
- ☐ Young's Winter Warmer (England)

The
Belgians

Abbey Dubbel

Iigh above the clanking bottling line at the brewery inside the Trappist abbey of Westmalle hangs an array of acoustic panels to deaden the noise. Wouldn't want to disturb the monks, who spend about seven hours a day praying in church. "Sometimes," said Marleen Hurdak, a spokeswoman for the brewery, "the monks tell us to just slow down."

Slow down? Right. They wouldn't be so contemplative if they weren't required to deny themselves the earthly pleasure of their brewery's heavenly Westmalle Dubbel. Those of us on the outside know that a single sinful taste of its malty body will tempt you to indulge in one creamy goblet after the next. You pause only a moment, letting the strong ale percolate through all your senses: hints of fruit and light spice in the nose, a sweet, full body in your mouth, and of course that blessed warm buzz of feel-good alcohol all over.

And then you jump right back in for another, succumbing to wanton desire. *Holy mother of God!*

Tiny Westmalle is thought to have invented the variety some 80 years ago, and today it is one of Belgium's defining styles. When someone says he likes Belgian beer, almost certainly what he means is dubbel. Corsendonk, Affligem, Maredsous, Grimbergen—some of the most cherished names in Belgian brewing are known primarily for their dubbels.

Dubbel is the Dutch word for double, a name that comes from the relative level of the original gravity—or density—of its wort, the traditional standard for measuring and taxing European beer. (Contrary to popular belief, it's not double the strength of a blonde, nor does it necessarily contain double the malt, nor does it refer to double fermentation.) Typically, brewers use pale pilsner malt, then add amber and caramel malts for color.

Traditionally, Belgian candi sugar is used to fortify its strength without adding more body. It provides a touch of sweetness and, most importantly, is responsible for that gorgeous pillowy head.

Like so many other Belgian ales, hops are not a big deal, typically unassertive, just enough to provide balance and only a hint of spice character, perhaps Styrian Goldings or Saaz.

So where does it get its fruity zip? Belgian yeast, naturally—probably two or three different strains, depending on the brewery. Dubbel is fermented at fairly warm temps to produce those fruity (raisin, apricot) esters.

For Gene Muller of Flying Fish Brewing in New Jersey, whose Belgian Abbey Dubbel was one of the earliest American versions of the style, it's the malt that truly defines this style. "You drink a dubbel, and what

Abbey Dubbel

Aroma: Rich malt with fruity esters,

Flavor: Medium to full body with complex malty sweetness.

Bitterness: 15-25 IBUs.

Strength: 6-7.5% abv.

you want is a nice malt character with a hint of, say, plum or almond," Muller said. "You don't want those phenolics that give you banana or clove. It's much more fruity…

"You want subtle flavors, something that you can drink with good food. With a lot of Belgian beers, you get all those extreme tastes. That's not the case with dubbel. There's nothing overwhelming. There's a lot of things you can read into it, but it never hits you over the head."

Quiet, full of meaning, pure in spirit, crafted with honest labor—the monks at Westmalle wouldn't have it any other way.

Abbey Dubbel Checklist

□ 21ˢᵗ Amendment Monk's Blood

□ Abita Abbey

□ Achel 8 Bruin (Belgium)

□ Affligem Dubbel (Belgium)

□ Allagash Double Ale

□ Andelot Cuvee Angelique (Belgium)

□ Anderson Valley Brother David's

□ Blue Moon Winter Abbey Ale

□ Boaks Two Blind Monks

□ Bornem Dubbel (Belgium)

□ Brewer's Art Resurrection

□ Captain Lawrence St. Vincent's

□ Chimay Premiere (Belgium)

□ Corsendonk Abbey Brown Ale (Belgium)

□ Flying Fish Belgian Abbey Dubbel

□ Goose Island Pere Jacques

□ Green's Endeavor (England)

□ Grimbergen Dubbel (Belgium)

□ Halve Maan Brugse Zot (Belgium)

□ La Trappe Dubbel (Netherlands)

□ Lost Abbey Lost & Found

□ Maredsous 8 (Belgium)

□ New Belgium Abbey Belgian Style Ale

□ **Ommegang Abbey Ale**

□ Petrus Dubbel (Belgium)

□ St Bernardus Prior 8 (Belgium)

□ St. Feuillien Brune (Belgium)

□ St. Martin Brune (Belgium)

□ St. Sebastiaan Dark (Belgium)

□ Slaghmuylder Witkap-Pater Dubbel (Belgium)

□ 't Smisje Dubbel (Belgium)

□ Steenbrugge Dubbel Bruin (Belgium)

□ Sterkens Dubbel (Belgium)

□ Val-Dieu Brune (Belgium)

□ Van den Bossche Pater Lieven Bruin (Belgium)

□ **Westmalle Dubbel (Belgium)**

□ Westvleteren 8 (Belgium)

Belgian IPA

Belgian Indian pale ale must be some kind of whacked-out test tube experiment in ethnic crossbreeding. Like French-Icelandic cuisine or an Irish-Samoan middle linebacker, the hybrid sounds positively alien, yet weirdly compelling.

You think Belgian, you think off-center, idiosyncratic styles. Funky lambic, sour red ale, malt bombs made by secretive Trappist monks.

Hops? In Belgium they're more apt to chew the bitter plants than toss them to the brew kettle. Coriander, dried orange peels—that's what they use in Louvain to spice beer, right?

And, yet, here we have it: a hoppy ale invented by British imperialists, perfected by tattooed Californians and uniquely adapted by country that reveres the Smurfs as timeless art.

Crack open a bottle and you don't know whether to laugh or pucker up.

Houblon Chouffe, perhaps the most widely known, looks like a classic tripel, bright and golden with a pillowy head that leaves behind its trademark lace pattern. Bring it up to your mouth for a sip, and instead of that spicy yeast kick in the nose, you get the telltale aroma of grass and citrus.

A jug leaves you confused, astonished, intrigued. Sweet and tingly with a hint of banana, it'll remind you of the brewery's flagship, La Chouffe. But then, a subtle bitterness fills your palate. It's not front and forward, like a more assertive west coast IPA; it's less obvious, as if someone tucked Pliny the Elder under a pile of warm blankets.

Take another sip and you find yourself asking: Why aren't there more Belgian beers like this?

It's not as if hops are completely unknown in Belgium. They are widely cultivated in the north, in western Flanders, and some well-known brands—Orval, for example—are famous for their hops. But an American hophead wandering into a Brussels café will never find a chalkboard listing IBU content.

Indeed, Hildegard Van Ostaden, the inventive brewer at De Leyerth who helped kick off the Belgian IPA trend a few years ago with her masterpiece Urthel Hop-It, didn't discover the wonder of hops till she visited America.

"I think the first really hoppy beer I tried was in Seattle, at Elysian Brewing," she told me. "Then I completely fell in love with Stone Arrogant Bastard. I became a huge fan of American IPAs. Each time I travel to the U.S., I get really addicted to the hops.

> ### Belgian IPA
>
> **Aroma:** Citrus hops with a biscuit-like malt balance.
>
> **Flavor**: Spicy with a notable yeast character, firmly hopped.
>
> **Bittnerness**: 60-100+ IBUs.
>
> **Strength:** 6-12% abv.
>
>

"So I thought, maybe I should try to make something like that."

More than a few beer traditionalists doubt that Belgian IPA is a bona fide style. There are few examples of the style and no firm brewing guidelines. Nearly every hoppy

Belgian, whether dubbel, blonde, abbey or even wild ale, seemingly qualifies for the rubric.

But those who get lost in that debate risk missing the marvel of Belgian IPAs.

Next to Germany and England, no other country has had a bigger impact on American craft beer scene than Belgium. Untold American brewers have spent hours upon hours attempting to brew clones of Duvel, Chimay and Saison Dupont. With so many cloudy wheat beers flowing from taps these days, one could argue that the most influential beer to hit these shores in the last 50 years is none other than Pierre Celis's Hoegaarden.

And now with the emergence of Belgian IPAs, at long last, America is returning the favor.

Belgian IPA Checklist

- ☐ **Achouffe Houblon Chouffe** (Belgium)
- ☐ Ale Asylum Bedlam
- ☐ Alternatief Bitter Truth (Belgium)
- ☐ Allagash Hugh Malone
- ☐ Alvinne Gaspar (Belgium)
- ☐ Bullfrog Houblonium P38
- ☐ Cathedral Square Hail Mary
- ☐ Charlevoix Vobiscum Lupulus (Canada)
- ☐ Clipper City Dubbel Cannon
- ☐ Clown Shoes Tramp Stamp
- ☐ Contreras Valeir Extra (Belgium)
- ☐ Coronado Hoppy Daze IPA
- ☐ De Ranke XX Bitter (Belgium)
- ☐ De Struise Ignis Et Flamma (Belgium)
- ☐ Duvel Tripel Hop (Belgium)
- ☐ **Flying Dog Raging Bitch**
- ☐ Furthermore Makeweight
- ☐ Gouden Carolus Hopsinjoor (Belgium)
- ☐ Great Divide Belgica
- ☐ Green Flash Le Freak
- ☐ Hill Farmstead E.
- ☐ Kuhnhenn Aldebaran
- ☐ Karl Strauss Blackball
- ☐ Lefebvre Hopus (Belgium)
- ☐ Midnight Sun Mayhem
- ☐ Musketiers Troubadour Magma (Belgium)
- ☐ New Belgium Lips of Faith Belgo IPA
- ☐ New Holland Farmhouse Hatter Belgian IPA
- ☐ Phillips Hoperation Tripel Cross (Canada)
- ☐ Peace Tree Hop Wranger
- ☐ Poperings Hommel Bier (Belgium)
- ☐ Rock Art American-Belgo Style IPA
- ☐ Stone Cali-Belgique
- ☐ 't Smisje IPA+ (Belgium)
- ☐ Terrapin Monk's Revenge
- ☐ Tyranena La Femme Amère
- ☐ Urthel Hop-It (Belgium)
- ☐ Van den Bossche Buffalo Belgian Bitter (Belgium)
- ☐ Van Steenberge Piraat (Belgium)
- ☐ Vivant Triomphe
- ☐ White Birch Hooksett Ale
- ☐ Victory Wild Devil

Biere de Champagne

If beer doesn't watch out, it's going to turn itself into wine. Already, beer has assimilated wine's bottles and corks, its grapes (Midas Touch, Cantillon Vigneronne) and even its place at the dinner table. Now beer is expropriating one of wine's most sacred rituals, the high art of *methode Champenoise*.

A couple of Belgian brewers—Bosteels and Landtsheer—are doing it, and so is an Oregon micro, Golden Valley.

Pop! Here comes a whole new beer style, known as Biere de Champagne or Biere Brut.

In truth, this style's a stretch because it's defined almost solely by its method of production, not by its ingredients and only marginally by the flavor and character of the final product.

But what a method. After bottling, the beer is refermented with a secondary dose of Champagne yeast. The bottles are aged on their sides, tilted toward the cap to allow the sediment to settle. Over months, they're twisted firmly to loosen the sediment from the sides (a process called riddling or *remuage*). Finally, the bottle necks are exposed to a cold brine mixture to flash-freeze the liquid so that a small block of sediment is expelled (*disgorgement*).

The result is a clean, sparkling, bubbly beer that drinks much like Champagne.

Indeed, the two best-known makers of Biere Brut have unabashedly drawn a parallel between their products and that rarified grape juice we sip on New Year's Eve. DeuS (Brut Des Flandres) makes such a big deal about the similarities, the Bosteels brewery goes to all the trouble of shipping the bottles to the Champagne region, where they're conditioned side by side with the real thing. The original DeuS label looked so much like the famous Dom

Perignon, Bosteels was compelled to re-design it under threat of a lawsuit. Meanwhile, Landtsheer once called its Malheur Bière Brut the "Veuve-Clicquot of the beer world" till it, too, was reportedly forced to back down.

In America, wine hasn't gotten so bent out of shape by beer's incursions. Golden Valley brewer Mark Vickery even credits the nearby Argyle winery with helping him refine the conditioning method for his IPA VS Brut.

It's a double India Pale Ale with about 8.5 percent alcohol that is first aged in the winery's used Chardonnay barrels for a month. Then it's bottled using *methode Champenoise*. "You get this Champagne character with layers of oak and hops—a real lingering hop finish," Vickery said.

Yes, it's a lot of effort. But as Vickery said, "My God, if you're going to be a brewer, especially here in the Northwest, you've really got to show yourself."

Fair enough—beer is evolving into something

> ### Biere de Champagne
>
> **Aroma**: Sweet, delicate and lightly fruity.
>
> **Flavor**: Effervescent, low bitterness, dry finish.
>
> **Bitterness**: 5-30 IBUs.
>
> **Strength**: 10-15% abv.
>
>

better because of that kind of attitude. But in the off-chance that the French threaten a lawsuit for big-footing their hallowed turf, beer might consider coming up with another name for this style.

How 'bout Extreme Bottle-Conditioned Ale?

Biere de Champagne Checklist

- □ **Bosteels DeuS— Brut Des Flandres** (Belgium)
- □ Boston Beer Infinium
- □ Charlevoix Dominus Vobiscum Brut (Canada)
- □ Cobra Krait Prestige (England)
- □ Dominus Vobiscum Brut (Canada)
- □ Eisenbahn Lust (Brazil)
- □ Eisenbahn Lust Prestige (Brazil)
- □ Kasteel Cru (France)
- □ Kasteel Cru Rose (France)
- □ Krait Prestige (England)
- □ Malheur Bière Brut (Belgium)
- □ Malheur Bruit Noir (Belgium)
- □ Malheur Cuvee Royale (Belgium)
- □ Midnight Sun Jupiter
- □ Mikkeller Nelson Sauvignon (Denmark)
- □ Rouget de Lisle Cristal des Grandvaux (France)

Biere de Mars

Here's a modest proposal. Actually, why mince words? It's more of a criminal conspiracy. But never mind, because my motive is sincere and the mark couldn't be easier.

It's France.

Here's the setup: Every year at the start of March, a handful of French brewers release a special beer to mark the coming change of seasons. It's called *Biere de Mars*, which is French for March beer. There's a bunch of hype. Cafés put up signs announcing the arrival of the malty, slightly hoppy brew from Meteor, Kronenbourg, Fischer and a few other breweries. It's all very reminiscent of the campaign promoting the coming of a certain overrated wine on the third Thursday of November: *Le Beaujolais Nouveau est arrivé!*

Only, this is beer and the French are, well, French, so they don't pay much attention to it all.

I say, while they're over there sipping their Chablis, we just sneak in and steal their Biere de Mars. Heck, we don't even have to sneak through customs. All we need is enough American brewers to start making the style, creating their own, distinctive version, and it'll be ours before the French know what hit 'em.

Why the foul play? Well, let's face it, though many of us enjoy those hearty ales of winter, the majority of Americans still don't reach for the keg in earnest till the warmer months. Biere de Mars can be our own American tradition. We might have to change the name (Spring Beer?), but it would be an ale our breweries ceremoniously release on March 1 each year, to officially kick off the beer-drinking season in style.

What kind of beer are we talking about here? Technically, it's a farmhouse ale, a specialty from Belgium and Northern France that was originally brewed mainly for sustenance, not commercial sales. Little is known about origin of Biere de Mars, but experts believe it was made in mid-winter with grains from the fall harvest, including wheat. Because cask cellars would be colder, fermentation was slower. It would age for six, eight weeks before it was released to welcome the new season.

I know, it sounds a lot like another springtime beer that American brewers already make—bock. But bock is a German lager, fairly beholden to strict style guidelines. Biere de Mars is an ale with few of those restrictive specs.

At Ommegang in New York, for example, former brewer Randy Thiel said he had no clear idea of the style when he tackled it once for a festival. "I just wanted something with a nice, fiery orange color to it with a big, beautiful white head." He,

Bière de Mars

Aroma: Herbal hops, distinctive earthiness.

Flavor: Slight fruitness with dry finish.

Bitterness: 18-30 IBUs.

Strength: 6-8.5% abv.

like Peter Bouckaert at Colorado's New Belgium, even added a touch of funky wild yeast, to give their versions a touch of sourness.

It's not complete anarchy, but there's enough room here to allow America's innovative brewers to show their chops.

And that might've been the whole idea behind the beer in the first place, said Phil Markowski of Southampton Brewing in New York, who wrote the authoritative

Farmhouse Ales: Culture and Craftsmanship in the European Tradition. Said Markowski: "Brewers would be especially proud of their Biere de Mars. It might be their best beer of season, possibly due to fact that they were trying to get people thinking about beer again after a long winter."

Now, is that such a crime?

Bière De Mars Checklist

☐ Bières 23 Bière De Mars (France)

☐ Flying Dog Avante Garde

☐ Jenlain Bière De Mars (France)

☐ Jolly Pumpkin Bière de Mars

☐ **La Choulette Bière De Mars** (France)

☐ La Rouget de Lisle Bière de Mars (France)

☐ Meteor Bière de Mars (France)

☐ New Belgium Lips of Faith—Biere de Mars

☐ Ommegang Bière De Mars

☐ Sornin Biere de Mars (France)

☐ Southampton Biere de Mars

Faro

You know those Belgian lambics that are all the rage these days? Beer fans rhapsodize about their complex character, their funky aroma, their tart flavor produced through the vagaries of spontaneous fermentation. The brewers who make them are worshipped as artisans, and highly valued bottles are collected and traded. It is so special, the style is now a protected appellation that can be produced only in a tiny region along the Senne River southwest of Brussels.

It's worth noting,though, that lambic wasn't always so beloved.

As recently as 25 years ago, Belgian lambic was largely regarded as beer gone bad. The French, in particular, often raised their Gallic noses in disdain at the beers from the north, complaining about their unusual flavor. The unusual beer was evidence—along with the grim architecture of Brussels, the harsh climate of the North Sea and the eel-centric cuisine of Antwerp—of Belgium's inferiority.

Even the Belgians themselves acknowledge that lambic takes some getting used to. They blend vintages to soften the edges, they add fruit—cherries, raspberries, raisins—to mask the off-flavors. And when all else fails, they dump pounds of sugar into the barrel to create a variety known as Faro.

It is a low-alcohol "small" beer made from secondary runnings from the mash tun, a process akin to re-using the grinds in your Mr. Coffee. The grain bill is typically about one-third unmalted wheat, and aged hops are added for preservation, not bitterness. Like any lambic, it is fermented in an open vat, then allowed to turn sour in the barrel. After some months, it is blended with fresh beer and sugar, perhaps some herbs. And then still more water to further weaken the blend to 3 percent alcohol or so.

In its heyday, Faro was the go-to drink of Belgium.

Belgians would spend hours in the cafe, rattling the dice throughout their beloved games of *mort subite* (sudden death), draining glass upon glass of Faro. It was light and refreshing and, French snobs notwithstanding, a pleasant respite. It was a drink that a child could handle without risk of falling over in a stupor. (Even today, it is not uncommon to spot a 10-year-old in Brussels' family-friendly cafes, happily stirring sugar into a glass of Faro as if it were iced tea.)

Yet, even in these days of renewed interest in artisanal Belgian styles, Faro is a rarity. Only a handful of breweries produce the style, and few of them ship it across the Atlantic.

Some versions, like De Troch Chapeau, are exceptionally sweet and reminiscent of Mott's Apple Juice. Others, like Lindemans Faro Lambic, balance that sweetness with the tartness produced by those wild yeast strains. After a glass, adjectives like "goaty" or "barnyard" come to mind.

Faro

Aroma: Sweet, caramel with funky undertones reminiscent of unwashed sweat socks.

Flavor: Sweet up front with a tart, crisp, green-apple finish.

Bitterness: 11-20 IBUs.

Strength: 2.5—4% abv.

Which, 150 years ago, was not exactly high praise.

The poet Charles Baudelaire held a special contempt for Faro in the mid-19th century.

In a letter to his mother during a stay in Brussels, he complained of "three months of continual diarrhea, broken occasionally by unbearable constipation" which he attributed to "the climate and the use of Faro."

In a pamphlet he titled, *Pauvre Belgique* ("Poor Belgium"), Baudelaire railed, "The Faro comes from that great big latrine, the Senne—a beverage extracted from the city's carefully sorted excrement. Thus it is that, for centuries, the city has drunk its own urine."

Which only underscores a basic truth of drinking: One man's pleasure is another man's piss.

Faro Checklist

☐ **Boon Faro** (Belgium)

☐ Cantillon Faro (Belgium)

☐ De Troch Chapeau Faro Lambic (Belgium)

☐ Drie Fonteinen Straffe Winter (Belgium)

☐ Girardin Dominicus (Belgium)

☐ Girardin Faro 1882 (Belgium)

☐ Lindemans Faro Lambic (Belgium)

☐ Mort Subite Faro (Belgium)

☐ St. Louis Premium Faro (Belgium)

☐ Timmermans Tradition Faro Lambic (Belgium)

Gueuze

Back in the early 2000's, Christian Heim, then head brewer at Lancaster Brewing in Pennsylvania, was training an assistant when they found themselves with a batch of wheat beer that had plainly gone south. "The flavor was off, there was some sort of infection," he said. "We had a whole tank of it, and I didn't want to dump it."

This would be neither the first nor the last time a professional brewer would try to make the best of a foul-up.

They rounded up some Lactobacillus bacteria and some wild yeast cultures (Heim doesn't remember the specifics), inoculated some fresh beer, and tossed that into the batch. Over the next four years, as the batch sat in the tank, he'd feed it from time to time with still more beer containing lacto or some oddball yeast strain.

"For the longest time it was a joke," Heim said. "It made vinegar taste mild, it was so sharp."

Eventually, he kegged it and let it sit in the brewery's attic, where it was either freezing cold or smoking hot. "I was always waiting to hear explosions up there," Heim laughed.

The kegs never blew. And what started out as a completely undrinkable beer slowly began to mellow. The sharp, acrid bite backed off, the flavor matured—damn, it was pretty good.

Anyone who has ever puckered after a tart, funky swallow of Cantillon, for example, will recognize what happened. Old, sour beer had been blended with fresh beer, allowed to re-ferment with a form of wild yeast and age in a barrel.

Heim, who labeled it "Old Sourpuss," had created his own version of gueuze.

Not exactly, of course.

In Belgium's Zenne Valley south of Brussels, where the original is made, lambic makers brew batches with pilsner malt and unmalted wheat. Then it's left to chill overnight in a large, open vessel known as a cool ship, to be exposed to ambient yeast strains and bacteria.

As with the "terroir" of wine-making regions, the aroma and flavor of this unusual beer is a direct result of the place in which it was brewed. Gueuze makers expose their beer to whatever yeast and other micro-organisms might inhabit their brewery. Some famously protect even the cobwebs, fearing any change in the environment will adversely affect the character.

The process sounds as haphazard as Heim's, but there's little left to chance.

Three-year-old batches are expertly blended with new lambic, which kicks off another round of fermentation before bottling. Barrels are further blended to create, for example, the distinctive earthy flavor of Drie Fonteinen Oud Gueuze or the locker room aroma of Hanssens Oude Gueuze.

Gueuze

Aroma: A funky barnyard waft with a touch of acidic fruit.

Flavor: A challenging, upfront acidic sourness with green-apple notes smoothes out for a dry, refreshing finish.

Bitterness: 0-10 IBUs.

Strength: 5-8% abv.

So, while Pennsylvania-made Old Sourpuss might've been made in much the same way as authentic gueuze, it presumably could never match the Belgian original.

Or could it?

Today, dozens of American brewers have experimented with the style, usually employing pre-packaged doses of the Zenne Valley's famous Brettanomyces bruxellensis yeast strain, believed by some to be the real source of all that funkiness. Others, like Lost Abbey, age beer in barrels inoculated with Brett to produce a tart, fruity complexity Meanwhile both Jolly Pumpkin and Allagash have produced lambics that were spontaneously fermented in open vessels—a first for U.S. craft breweries.

As with so many other styles, someday, perhaps, there will be an official American-style gueuze.

As for Heim's "gueuze," well, there are still 30 or 40 half barrels left. But don't expect a re-creation. Said Heim: "It was a Frankenstein from the get-go."

Gueuze Checklist

- ☐ Belle Vue Gueuze (Belgium)
- ☐ Boon Moriau Gueuze (Belgium)
- ☐ Boon Oude Geuze Mariage Parfait (Belgium)
- ☐ Boon Oude Gueuze (Belgium)
- ☐ Breughel Gueuze (Canada)
- ☐ Cantillon 50°N-4°E (Belgium)
- ☐ **Cantillon Gueuze 100% Lambic** (Belgium)
- ☐ Cantillon Lou Pepe (Belgium)
- ☐ Chapeau Xmas Gueuze (Belgium)
- ☐ De Dochter L'enfant Terrible (Belgium)
- ☐ De Neve Gueuze (Belgium)
- ☐ Drie Fonteinen Doesjel (Belgium)
- ☐ Drie Fonteinen Oud Gueuze (Belgium)
- ☐ Geuze De Cam (Belgium)
- ☐ Girardin Gueuze—Black Label (Belgium)
- ☐ **Hanssens Oude Gueuze** (Belgium)
- ☐ HORALs Oude Geuze Mega Blend (Belgium)
- ☐ Jacobins Gueuze (Belgium)
- ☐ Jolly Pumpkin Lambicus Dexterius
- ☐ Lindemans Gueuze (Belgium)
- ☐ Lindemans Gueuze Cuvee Rene (Belgium)
- ☐ Mort Subite Unfiltered Gueuze (Belgium)
- ☐ New Glarus R & D Gueuze
- ☐ Oud Beersel Oude Gueuze (Belgium)
- ☐ Schoune Ma Ptite Gueuze (Canada)
- ☐ St. Louis Gueuze Fond Tradition (Belgium)
- ☐ Timmermans Tradition Gueuze Lambic (Belgium)
- ☐ Upstream Gueuze-Lambic
- ☐ Vicardin Tripel Gueuze (Belgium)

Oud Bruin/Flemish Brown Ale

A few years ago during a visit to De Proef Brouwerij outside of Ghent, Belgium, a group of American beer enthusiasts—a couple of importers, a bar owner and one or two others—sat around a table with famed brewing engineer Dirk Naudts to conduct one of the odder tasting sessions I've encountered.

The goal was to design a new brand for the U.S. market, and various ingredients were displayed for sampling. There were hops and some grains, naturally, but what caught everyone's attention was the dish of grayish-white powder passed furtively from one to the next. Each would pluck a bit from the dish and place it on his tongue, almost as a dare.

Naudts flashed the nasty smile of a man about to pull off a practical joke. Within seconds, our mouths were as dry as bleached leather, our cheeks collapsed into a face-contorting pucker, every last molecule of moisture sucked away.

The powder was pure, utterly sour lactic acid, the granular essence of a unique beer style: Flemish Brown Ale.

Also know as Oud Bruin, the variety is marked by a distinct piquant tartness that is produced by Lactobacillus, an aggressive bacteria that infects the ale during fermentation.

Lactic acid bacterium is a big troublemaker in the brewhouse, turning perfectly good beer into lemons. Occurring naturally and invisible to the naked eye, it was a mystery till Pasteur showed up with his microscope in the 1860s. Before that, a man (or in the case of the infamous Pendle witches, a woman) could be hanged for sour beer.

But as the brewers of Oudenaarde in Belgium's East Flanders know well, Lactobacillus can be a good thing.

At breweries such as Liefman's and Roman, the bacteria is welcomed into the fermentation tanks, added to the yeast to produce an earthy funk over the months of conditioning. Though it is not spontaneous fermentation, as in the lambic breweries of Payottenland, the effect is much the same. The final flavor is achieved through meticulous blending, with batches of young and aged beer combined to round out the edges, soften the tartness and produce smooth complexity.

(Though made in much the same manner, Flemish Red Ale such as Rodenbach, is regarded as a distinct style by some experts because it receives its lactic shock through aging in wooden vats.)

Liefman's Goudenband (Gold Ribbon), now produced by Duvel Moortgat, is perhaps the benchmark; Michael Jackson once called it, "Surely the best brown ale in the world." Its bottles, wrapped in paper, pour a dark ruby-brown, a clue to its rich malt undercarriage. The first

Oud Bruin-Flanders Brown Ale

Aroma: Rich malt character with distinct fruity esters.

Flavor: Dried fruit (raisin, plum, fig) with an edge of sourness.

Bitterness: 20-25 IBUs.

Strength: 4-8% abv.

swallow is lightly sweet and fruity up front with Pilsner, crystal and roasted malt, while the finish is acetic and complex with little evidence of hops. Let the bottle sit in your cellar a few months, and the tartness only grows.

It is an acquired taste, it's true. Novice tonsils, trained on pure lagers, might gag on the sour wonder of lactic acid.

Slowly, though, beer fans are re-discovering the wonders of sour beer. Today, the Great American Beer Festival recognizes no fewer than four separate sour beer judging categories. Colorado's Avery Brewing now hosts the annual Boulder SourFest, an event that attracts a share of American-made Oud Bruin.

But a roundtable tasting of lactic powder? Take my parched word for it: It'll be a long time till that catches on.

Oud Bruin/Flanders Brown Ale Checklist

☐ Bios Blaamse Bourgogne (Belgium)

☐ Bockor Bellegems Bruin (Belgium)

☐ De Struise Earthmonk (Belgium)

☐ Deschutes The Dissident

☐ Goose Island Madame Rose

☐ Haandbryggeriet Haandbakk (Denmark)

☐ Ichtegems Oud Bruin (Belgium)

☐ Jackie O's Chunga's Old Bruin

☐ Kuhnhenn Olde Brune

☐ **Liefman's Goudenband** (Belgium)

☐ Liefman's Oud Bruin (Belgium)

☐ Lost Abbey Red Poppy

☐ Monk's Café Flemish Sour (Belgium)

☐ Ommegang Zuur

☐ **Petrus Aged Ale** (Belgium)

☐ Petrus Oud Bruin (Belgium)

☐ Portsmouth Sour Brune

☐ Riva Vondel (Belgium)

☐ The Bruery Oude Tart

☐ Timmermans Bourgogne Des Flandres Brune (Belgium

☐ **Verhaeghe Vichte Duchesse de Bourgogne** (Belgium)

Saison

The centuries-old story of saison—the classic Belgian farmhouse ale—is something out of a fairy tale.

Made with sparkling spring water and the bounty of the harvest, it would be brewed during the winter, then carefully cellared and aged to develop an uncommonly flavorful character to be enjoyed during the summer when it was too warm to make beer. Thus, smiling workers in dusty overalls could look to the end of another blissful day in the fields, when the farmer's innocently seductive daughter might pour them a cool, refreshing cup of those wondrous suds.

Why, with the blessed ale to quench their thirst, the field hands would barely ask to be paid for their day's toil.

With every sip of saison, you can just taste the romance. Kind of makes you want to grab a hoe and volunteer at your local organic farm co-op.

Until you remember your 19th-century European history.

Let's see, the water was filthy with dysentery, the crops were withered from a beetle infestation, the farm had been pillaged by Napoleon's armies, the labor was indentured and the farmer's daughter had eight teeth.

But, damn, that beer was delicious!

The best saison is still made on the farm, albeit one that enjoys the modern conveniences of irrigation and gas-powered tractors. You know it as Saison Dupont. The brewery's small farm in Belgium's French-speaking Wallonia has been in operation since the mid-1700s, with a mere 12 employees and enough animals to produce a steady supply of cheese and eggs.

A walk through its fields in the cold fog of late winter gives you a hint of this beer's flavor. It's dense and bracing, with a hint of herbs and fruit in the air, not to mention that familiar farm-like funk. Moisten your maw with a freshly popped bottle of Saison Dupont and you understand how a beer can be the product of its environment. Pair it with cheese or fish or salad or chicken or… hell, it goes with almost anything.

Originally, farmhouses brewed their saison just once a year, in the winter with the last of the summer crop of barley, then allowed it to age a full season (saison is French for "season"). It would be made strong enough in alcohol to withstand the months of cellaring, but light enough to prevent the hired hands from drunkenly pawing the toothless daughter.

Saison

Aroma: Citrus-like with some spice.

Flavor: Fruity, slightly earthy with a peppery and pleasingly bitter kick.

Bitterness: 25-45 IBUs.

Strength: 5—8.5% abv.

At Dupont, they boast that the complexity of flavor is not the product of additional spices—just good, old East Kent Goldings hops and a house yeast.

The beer is still brewed in an antique open mash tun. It takes a laborious 11 hours to make just one batch, but the remainder of the process is much less tedious. Instead of conditioning the ale for months, a one-week fermentation is followed by two more weeks of maturation and another 6-8 weeks in the bottle before it's shipped.

A shocking departure from tradition? Yes, but I've found that even high-tech breweries tucked into American office parks can produce a passable—even world-class— saison.

At Clipper City in Baltimore, for example, the full-flavored Heavy Seas Red Sky at Night is made with a simple over-the-counter strain of Belgian farmhouse yeast, a big dose of wheat and a smidge of dry-hopping for aroma, not bitterness. "We want it sort of spicy, a little musty with a fullness of body," said brewer John Eugeni.

No fairy tales needed.

Saison Checklist

- ☐ Brooklyn Local 1
- ☐ Cigar City Guava Grove
- ☐ Dupont Avec Les Bon Vouex (Belgium)
- ☐ Dupont Foret
- ☐ Fantôme Saison (Belgium)
- ☐ Géants Saison Voisin (Belgium)
- ☐ Glazen Toren Saison d'Erpe-Mere (Belgium)
- ☐ Goose Island Sofie
- ☐ Great Divde Colette
- ☐ HaandBryggeriet Ardenne Blond (Norway)
- ☐ Heavy Seas Red Sky at Night
- ☐ Ithaca Ground Break
- ☐ Jandrain-Jandrenouille IV Saison (Belgium)
- ☐ Jolly Pumpkin Bam Bière
- ☐ North Coast Le Merle
- ☐ Ommegang Hennepin
- ☐ Pretty Things Jack D'Or
- ☐ **Saint Somewhere Saison Athene**
- ☐ Saison de Pipaix (Belgium)
- ☐ Saison De Silly (Belgium)
- ☐ **Saison Dupont** (Belgium)
- ☐ Sly Fox Saison Vos
- ☐ Smuttynose Farmhouse Ale
- ☐ Southampton Cuvee Des Fleurs
- ☐ Southampton Saison
- ☐ Surly CynicAle
- ☐ The Bruery Saison De Lente
- ☐ The Bruery Saison Rue
- ☐ The Lost Abbey Carnevale
- ☐ Thiriez XXtra (France)
- ☐ Troll Daü (Italy)
- ☐ Urthel Saisonnière (Belgium)
- ☐ Victory Helios
- ☐ Yards Saison

Tripel

How could such a grand style have such a generic name?

Tripel. Or Trippel. Or Triple. Or however you spell it, it's a bland and marginally apt description for a Belgian-style golden ale that combines distinctive aroma and flavor with a potent strength that—upon ingestion—tends to raise these very questions.

Tripel what? you might wonder after polishing off a 750 of sweetly smooth Chimay Cinq Cents. It's not three times the alcoholic strength of a basic beer, nor the gravity nor the malt nor the hops. It has nothing to do with its process of fermentation nor even its price.

It's merely a relative measurement that exists solely as a comparison to a less potent style, the Dubbel. How much stronger, who knows? It's like XXX movies, which I've determined upon careful examination do not contain exactly three times the penetration of your standard soft-core Cinemax porn.

Not that I'd suggest that the celibate monks who invented this stuff might have found inspiration in, say, "Gangbanger Coeds VI." All I'm saying is, with all that time on their hands, you'd think they'd come up with a better name.

Which, it turns out, they did; tripel was originally known as *Prima Melior*. It's Latin for "the best of the best"—the cup that the earliest monastic brewers reserved for the abbot and distinguished guests.

"*Secunda*"—the second best—was the everyday beer for the brothers. "*Tertia*" — the weakest — was offered to beggars and pilgrims. With *Prima Melior*, they provided a trinity of flavors that some experts believe may be the very genesis of our modern single (or blond), dubbel and tripel.

Stan Hieronymus, a leading expert on Trappist beer and author of *Brew Like a Monk,* points to the 9th-century St. Gall Monastery plan as evidence. The plan—a blueprint for an ideal monastery that was never built—depicts churches, houses, kitchens, bakeries, workshops, and even a building for bloodletting. It also shows three separate breweries (*bracitoria*), one each for paupers, monks and guests, each presumably making one of three different styles. As techniques improved over the centuries, Hieronymus says, brewers would've learned how to produce the three different beers from one brew-house, with second and third runnings from a single mash.

It's the first extraction of undiluted wort—stronger, sweeter, better—that would've created *Prima Melior.*

Today, Abbaye de Leffe packages a beer called Prima Melior which, with its dark, heavy body and anis and coriander spices, is probably pretty close to what those ancient monks were serving to visiting royalty. But it's not a Tripel as we know it today.

Tripel

Aroma: Complex array of spice and fruit, with low hops.

Flavor: Light malt underlies a tangy, fruity, bubbly body with a pleasing alcohol kick.

Bitterness: 20-40 IBUs.

Strength: 7.5-9.5% abv.

For that, we need to check in with the Trappist brewery at the Westmalle monastery in Belgium, which makes what is widely regarded as the style's benchmark. Strong, aromatic and notably blond beneath a big, billowing head of white foam, its medium body is positively effervescent. The alcohol gets a boost from the use of candi sugar, which also provides some honey or rum-like notes. It finishes dry, thanks to Saaz and Styrian Goldings.

As in many Belgian-style ales, it's the yeast that does the heavy lifting here. The primary fermentation is long and warm before it is re-fermented for five weeks in the bottle to produce an array of complex aromas and flavors.

It is an outstanding masterpiece, the product of superb craftsmanship and imagination. And Westmalle gave it the most ordinary of names—Tripel, a name that ultimately would be co-opted by other breweries to denote an entire, luxurious style.

Is that the best they could come up with?

Well, no. When Westmalle first released the beer in the 1930s, the monks labeled it "Superbier."

Lame.

Religious orders were much more immaginative back in the days of bloodletting.

Tripel Checklist

- ☐ Achel 8 Blond (Belgium)
- ☐ Affligem Tripel (Belgium)
- ☐ **Allagash Tripel Reserve**
- ☐ Bornem Tripel (Belgium)
- ☐ Boulevard Long Strange Tripel
- ☐ Brewer's Art Green Peppercorn
- ☐ Chimay Cinq Cents (Belgium)
- ☐ Corsendonk Abbey Pale Ale (Belgium)
- ☐ Dark Horse Sapient Trip
- ☐ De Dolle Dulle Teve (Belgium)
- ☐ De Ranke Guldenberg (Belgium)
- ☐ Flying Dog Kerberos
- ☐ Gouden Carolus Tripel (Belgium)
- ☐ Green Flash Trippel
- ☐ Kasteel Blond (Belgium)
- ☐ La Rullés Triple (Belgium)
- ☐ La Trappe Tripel (Netherlands)
- ☐ Maredsous 10 (Belgium)
- ☐ Middle Ages Tripel Crown
- ☐ Midnight Sun Panty Peeler
- ☐ New Belgium Trippel
- ☐ New Holland Black Tulip
- ☐ Petrus Gouden Tripel (Belgium)
- ☐ River Horse Tripel Horse
- ☐ Russian River Damnation
- ☐ Slaapmutske Triple Nightcap (Belgium)
- ☐ Sprecher Abbey Triple
- ☐ St. Bernardus Tripel (Belgium)
- ☐ St. Feuillien Triple (Belgium)
- ☐ Steenberge Augustijn (Belgium)
- ☐ Stoudt's Tripel
- ☐ The Bruery Trade Winds
- ☐ Tripel Karmeliet (Belgium)
- ☐ **Unibroue La Fin du Monde** (Canada)
- ☐ Val-Dieu Triple (Belgium)
- ☐ Victory Golden Monkey
- ☐ Watou Tripel (Belgium)
- ☐ **Westmalle Tripel** (Belgium)
- ☐ **Weyerbacher Merry Monks**
- ☐ Witkap Pater Tripel (Belgium)

Witbier

Lately, there's been a bizarre struggle over tap handles in my hometown, Philadelphia, and I suspect you've seen evidence of it at your local pub. Instead of going at each other's throats with clear, yellow lager, the Big 3 have been battling it out with a cache of surrogate brands that are the flavor/style/philosophical opposites of their flagships—namely, witbier.

Budweiser? Forget about it, Anheuser-Busch has hooked up with InBev and now its sales reps are pushing Hoegaarden. The guy in the Miller uniform is rolling in a keg of orange-flavored Leinenkugel's Sunset Wheat and the Coors truck has a fancy new paint job with a logo for Blue Moon.

White beer, folks. Opaque, hazy stuff with yeast thingies still floating around in the glass. Need I remind you that just a dozen years ago, Milwaukee tried to sell us something called Miller Clear?

The irony is all the more remarkable because witbier (or *blanche*, in French) was neary wiped out after World War I by those famously crisp, clean European-style lagers. The style goes back 500 years, to a period when beer was made with wheat and typically balanced not by hops, but by a blend of herbs and spices known as gruit. Brewers in the Flemish town of Leuven perfected the style, using spices and oranges that had been imported from the Dutch colony of Curacao. Modern brewing methods, the widespread use of hops and a fascination with golden lager conspired to force the white ale into near extinction.

Enter one of the heroes of the modern craft beer renaissance, a Belgian milkman named Pierre Celis. His story should be required reading for any beer fan, but here's the quick version: Longing for the forgotten style, he developed the recipe for Hoegaarden, opened his own brewery, watched it burn down, rebuilt it, sold out to a bigger brewery, moved to Texas, developed the recipe for Celis White, sold out to a bigger brewery, moved back to Belgium and started yet another brewery.

His witbier was delicious, refreshing and unique—and it caught the eye of scores of other brewers.

"I wasn't trying to imitate any particular beer," said Rob Tod, who made Allagash White his brewery's flagship in the mid-1990s, "but I loved the flavor and refreshment of Hoegaarden and Celis White."

Take one sip of witbier and your mouth is swimming in currents of spice and fruit, wheat and oats. In Samuel Adams White, you might detect hints of vanilla; in Flying Dog's Woody Creek White, it's pepper and cloves; in Blanche de Chambly, well, I can't put a finger on the spices.

"It evolves," Tod said of the style. "After a couple of sips, you should be asking yourself: What is that flavor? What is that spice? What is that yeast?"

Witbier

Aroma: Honey-like sweetness, a bit of spice with zesty citrus.

Flavor: Crisp, dry with a distinctive orange fruitiness.

Bitterness: 10-20 IBUs.

Strength: 4.5-5.5% abv.

While the answers may be as murky as the white beer itself, appreciation of the style is unmistakable. Everyone, from newbies to pros, finds something to like it witbier. Even BudMillerCoors could see that.

Witbier Checklist

- ☐ Abita Satsum Harvest Wit
- ☐ Alaskan White
- ☐ Allagash White
- ☐ Avery White Rascal
- ☐ Bavik Wittekerke (Belgium)
- ☐ Bell's Winter White Ale
- ☐ **Blanche de Bruxelles** a.k.a. Manneken Pis (Belgium)
- ☐ Blue Moon
- ☐ Blue Moon Grand Cru
- ☐ Boulevard ZÔN
- ☐ Caracole Troublette (Belgium)
- ☐ Cisco Grey Lady
- ☐ Dogfish Head Namaste
- ☐ Estrella Damm Inedit (Spain)
- ☐ Flying Dog Woody Creek
- ☐ Glazen Toren Jan de Lichte (Belgium)
- ☐ Great Lakes Holy Moses
- ☐ Gulpener Korenwolf (Netherlands)
- ☐ Harpoon UFO White
- ☐ Hitachino Nest White Ale (Japan)
- ☐ **Hoegaarden Original White Ale** (Belgium)
- ☐ Jacobsen Sommer Wit (Denmark)
- ☐ Jolly Pumpkin Calabaza Blanca
- ☐ Leinenkugel's Sunset Wheat
- ☐ Long Trail Belgian White
- ☐ Lost Coast Great White
- ☐ Middle Ages Swallow Wit
- ☐ New Belgium Mothership Wit
- ☐ New Holland Zoomer
- ☐ Ommegang Witte
- ☐ Philadelphia Brewing Walt Wit
- ☐ Samuel Adams White Ale
- ☐ Saranac Belgian White
- ☐ Shock Top Belgian White
- ☐ Smisje Vuuve (Belgium)
- ☐ **St. Bernardus Witbier** (Belgium)
- ☐ Sterkens White (Belgium)
- ☐ The Lost Abbey Witch's Wit
- ☐ Two Brothers Monarch White
- ☐ Unibroue Blanche de Chambly (Canada)
- ☐ Upland Wheat Ale
- ☐ Victory Whirlwind Witbier
- ☐ Weyerbacher Blanche

The
Americans

American Pale Ale

"The moment that American pale ale became its own style," said Steve Dressler, the brewmaster at Sierra Nevada Brewing, "was when Ken chose Cascades as the hops."

That would be Ken Grossman, Sierra Nevada's founder and one of the pioneers of modern American craft brewing. Dressler wasn't there at the fateful moment some 30 years ago when the brewery's flagship brand was created, but he's brewed enough American pale ale— probably more than anyone on the planet—to know that more than any ingredient, it's those distinctly fruity, piney hops that are the essence of this style.

Indeed, it wouldn't be an overstatement to suggest that the single most important ingredient in the entire modern American beer renaissance is Cascades hops.

Think about it—those sad, dark ages of, say, 10 B.C. (before Cascades). America was a land of bland, canned brands, too nondescript for words. The hops they used in domestic lagers were mainly for balance—not aroma or assertive flavor.

Cascades had been developed in the 1950s at Oregon State University, but it wouldn't be released for widespread use until the early '70s. There are reports that Coors was the first to use it in a mainstream beer, and Anchor used it in some brands as well.

But it was Grossman, a bicycle repairman who learned to brew as a teenager, who choose Cascades as the foundation of his entire brewing realm.

Bright, vital, seductive—those hops were, and still are, a revelation for beer lovers. Added in the final stages of brewing to accentuate their aroma, the hops boldly announce their arrival by smothering the schnoz with a fresh wallop of citrus and freshly cut grass. Their grapefruit-like flavor rides proudly above the malt, biting the palate in an unapologetically bitter finish.

In an era when American beer drinkers might've found Becks and Heineken a flavor challenge, the use of Cascades in Sierra Nevada Pale Ale was a balls-out statement of beer-making machismo. Even the pale ales or bitters that we were lucky enough to grab from the U.K.—Bass or Whitbread—didn't have SNPA's cojones. The Brits tended to accentuate the malt, relying on less aromatic English hops like Fuggles and East Kent Goldings.

"Going with Cascades," said Dressler, "was a bold move. It was an overpowering aromatic. You know, we didn't have any of these other aromatic hop varieties around. Amarillo, Simcoe— none of them existed."

Sierra Nevada Pale Ale (along with Anchor Steam, Sam Adams Boston Lager and Pete's Wicked Ale)

American Pale Ale

Aroma: Moderate to strong dry-hop aroma with citrusy character.

Flavor: High hop flavor, clean malt with crisp, refreshing hop finish.

Bitterness: 30-45 IBUs.

Strength: 4.5—6.5% abv.

would become an anchor of the American craft beer movement, inspiring 1,000 imitations among homebrewers and professionals alike. Who could resist an ale with Cascades? Not even Anheuser-Busch: When the brewery responsible for so many cookie-cutter, hop-castrated lagers over the decades finally got around to introducing

Budweiser American Ale in 2008, guess which hops variety it used.

And so this wasn't just about a single brand. It was about the creation of a distinctive style. An *American*-style pale ale.

It was as if Gambrinus himself—angered that this great brewing nation had lost its way—had thrust a lightning bolt toward Chico, California, and demanded, "Enough with the crappy lagers. Use Cascades, dammit!"

American Pale Ale Checklist

- ☐ Acme California Pale Ale
- ☐ Alesmith X
- ☐ **Anchor Liberty Ale**
- ☐ Anderson Valley Poleeko Gold Pale Ale
- ☐ Bear Republic XP
- ☐ Bell's Pale Ale
- ☐ Boulder Hazed & Infused
- ☐ Boulevard Pale Ale
- ☐ Budweiser American Ale
- ☐ Butternuts Porkslap Pale Ale
- ☐ Caldera Pale Ale
- ☐ Deschutes Mirror Pond
- ☐ Dogfish Head Shelter Pale Ale
- ☐ Firestone Walker Pale 31
- ☐ Flying Dog Doggie Style
- ☐ Founders Pale Ale
- ☐ Full Sail Pale Ale
- ☐ Geary's Pale Ale
- ☐ Great Divide Fresh Hop
- ☐ Great Lakes Burning River
- ☐ Half Acre Daisy Cutter
- ☐ Lambrate Ligera (Italy)
- ☐ Kona Fire Rock
- ☐ Lancaster Amish Four Grain
- ☐ Left Hand Jackman's

- ☐ Little Creatures Pale Ale (Australia)
- ☐ Matilda Bay Alpha Pale Ale (Australia)
- ☐ McAuslan Brewing St-Ambroise (Canada)
- ☐ Mendocino Blue Heron
- ☐ New Belgium Mighty Arrow
- ☐ New Glarus Moon Man
- ☐ **Oskar Blues Dale's Pale Ale**
- ☐ Otter Creek Pale Ale
- ☐ River Horse Hop Hazard
- ☐ **Sierra Nevada Pale Ale**
- ☐ Smuttynose Shoals Pale Ale
- ☐ Southern Star Pine Belt
- ☐ Southern Tier Phin & Matt's Extraordinary Ale
- ☐ Stoudt's American Pale Ale
- ☐ Sweetwater 420
- ☐ Three Floyds Alpha King
- ☐ Troegs Pale Ale
- ☐ Tuppers' Hop Pocket Ale
- ☐ Two Brothers The Bitter End
- ☐ Widmer Drifter Pale Ale
- ☐ Yards Philadelphia Pale Ale

American Pale Wheat

American brewers who dabble in wheat must feel some days like William Murray.

Who?

William Murray—a mostly forgettable character from 17th-century England who had the somewhat bad luck of being the boyhood pal of Charles I. It was Charles' father, King James I, who devised the philosophy of the "divine right of kings."

"The state of monarchy," James wrote, "is the supremest thing upon earth; for kings are not only God's lieutenants upon earth, and sit upon God's throne, but even by God himself are called gods."

Which is all well and good until it comes time to give the king's obnoxious son a well-deserved spanking. No one would dare lay a hand on the son of a god, right?

Instead, it was his friend, the unfortunate William Murray, who felt the lash. Charles won't eat his veggies, William gets a beating. Charlie sasses his nanny, William gets a shellacking.

Thus was born the entirely odious concept of the whipping boy.

Which only makes me wonder: Who made German hefeweizen the prince of beers?

For there can be no other explanation for the state of affairs that has left its erstwhile friend, American pale wheat beer, the whipping boy of beer styles.

No beer style gets flogged by beer freaks as often as American pale wheat (except, perhaps, for American light lager, which really has it coming). Beer drinkers (including myself) routinely shrug off the style and accuse U.S.

brewers of willful castration. Tart-tongued reviewers scoff: *"Where's the bleeping banana? Where's the clove?"*

A spokesman for Indiana's Three Floyds Brewery once told me that his company began brewing Gumballhead because "Nick Floyd [the founder] felt most American wheat beers basically sucked."

And Brooklyn Brewery's Garrett Oliver once told the New York Times that Widmer Hefeweizen—one of the top-selling wheat beers made in America—was "trading on the good name of an actual, established style to sell something that's different."

The difference is primarily in the yeast. Early American craft brewers like Widmer, hesitant to introduce a second strain into their brewhouse, often made wheat beer with the same house yeast they used for pale ale or other styles. The ale might look like a hefeweizen, but—without the telltale esters and phenols produced by classic German weizen yeast—it would smell and taste like something else.

American Pale Wheat Ale

Aroma: Grainy wheat with moderate hop character.

Flavor: Solid wheat with even-handed hops, may finish sweet or dry.

Bitterness: 15-30 IBUs.

Strength: 4-7% abv.

Which is exactly the reason American pale wheat evolved into a style of its own.

As Gordon Strong, president of the Beer Judge Certification Program told Stan Hieronymus in his guide, *Brewing with Wheat,* "Most people should know that you use a neutral American yeast in this style, but some people still get it wrong. Don't use a German weizen yeast."

Or, as the BJCP style guidelines stress, "The clove and banana aromas common to German hefeweizens are inappropriate."

While that difference may have prompted handwringing among some critics, it also led to a veritable explosion of American innovation. Unbound by German tradition, American wheat ales have evolved with a playful, varied spirit, from the immensely popular Samuel Adams Summer Ale (spiced with Grains of Paradise) to the aforementioned Gumballhead (spiked with ample Amarillo hops). They may be refreshing (Bells Oberon Ale) or sweet (Ithaca White Gold) or bracing (Southern Tier ÜberSun).

Rightly or wrongly, American wheat ale is the whipping boy for Bavarian hefeweizen... but it turns out that's not such a bad thing. After all, William Murray's suffering and loyalty eventually earned him a royal title and the deed to London's palatial Ham House.

And Charles I? Convicted of treason and beheaded before a mob.

American Pale Wheat Checklist

☐ Abita Wheat

☐ Anchor Summer Beer

☐ Anderson Valley High Rollers Wheat

☐ Appalachian Water Gap Wheat

☐ Arcadia Whitsun

☐ Bell's Oberon

☐ Big Rock Grasshopper

☐ Big Sky Montana Trout Slayer

☐ Boulder Sweaty Betty

☐ Bouleveard Unfiltered Wheat

☐ Breckenridge SummerBright

☐ Carlow Curim Gold (Ireland)

☐ Coney Island Albino Python

☐ Dundee Wheat

☐ Firestone Walker Solace

☐ Flossmoor Station Station Master

☐ Goose Island 312 Urban Wheat

☐ Harpoon UFO

☐ Highland Cattail Peak

☐ Honey Moon Summer Ale

☐ Ithaca White Gold

☐ Kona Wailua Wheat

☐ Lagunitas A Little Sumpin' Sumpin'

☐ Lazy Magnolia Indian Summer

☐ Magic Hat Circus Boy

☐ Michelob Hop Hound

☐ New Belgium Sunshine Wheat

☐ North Coast Blue Star

☐ Odell Easy Wheat

☐ Otter Creek Summer Ale

☐ Pyramid Haywire

☐ Redhook Sunrye

☐ **Samuel Adams Summer Ale**

☐ Saranac Summer Ale

☐ Schlafly Hefeweizen

☐ Smuttynose Summer Weizen

☐ Southern Tier 422

☐ Southern Tier Hop Sun

☐ Stevens Point Horizon Wheat

☐ Three Floyds Gumballhead

☐ Tommy Knocker Jack Whacker

☐ Troegs Dreamweaver Wheat

☐ Wachusett Summer

☐ **Widmer Hefeweizen**

Barleywine

Once upon a time in the aisles of an American beer store, there was a knucklehead who, upon seeing a label for Barleywine, picked his nose and bought the bottle, certain that (despite the fact, as mentioned in the first clause of this sentence, he was in a BEER store) he was purchasing *wine*.

He got it home, cracked it open and found suds, not grape. Perhaps he complained to the store, maybe he hired a lawyer. Whatever, the federal government—duly empowered to protect American consumers from the idiocy of their dullest brothers—now requires that all bottles of this miscreant beverage be labeled not as barleywine, but as "Barleywine-Style Ale."

OK, before I go off the deep end, I'll acknowledge this is a pet peeve—and not just because fair play should mandate that Chablis and Chardonnay be accurately labeled as "White Grape-Style Wine."

Instead, it is history that informs this cause. Calling it Barleywine-Style Ale is redundant and demeaning because barleywine (or barley wine) is civilization's original name for beer.

It's what the earliest Egyptians called their brew of choice; ancient artifacts describe the process of making a "wine" from barley. Four hundred years before the birth of Christ, the Greeks were using the same description—"zythos" in their tongue. Aristotle, a bugger for the bottle, even documented its effects on the inebriated" While wine drinkers were apt to fall in any direction, he said, barleywine drunks could depend on falling on their backs.

I haven't read of any recent studies on the phenomenon, but certainly barleywine (Victory Old Horizontal, perhaps?) has been the culprit in more than a few stumbles. It is a beer of strength—two, three times the alcohol of your typical lager.

The English get the credit for the modern incarnation of the style, with the introduction of Bass No. 1 around 1870. (There are still ancient bottles of the stuff floating around, and White Shield Brewery in Burton—on the grounds of the original Bass brewery—periodically re-creates the original in extremely limited supplies.)

As with many styles, it was Fritz Maytag—the washing machine scion who resurrected Anchor Brewing and ignited the craft beer renaissance— who gave America its first taste of barleywine. In the mid-'70s, he remembers, he toured England in pursuit of traditional ales. "We saw the most charming old-fashioned breweries that existed," he told me. "But I was very disappointed with what I saw and tasted—lots of antiquity, but little tradition. No all-malt ale, no dry-hopped ale. The only thing we found intriguing was the barleywine, from Watney's.

> ### Barleywine
>
> **Aroma:** Intense, fruit-like malt, resiny hops.
>
> **Flavor**: Extreme malt character leaning toward intense hop bitterness.
>
> **Bitterness**: 50-120 IBUs.
>
> **Strength**: 8-15% abv.
>
>

"So we brewed a barleywine with all malt. And that became Old Foghorn in the fall of 1975."

Maytag's version kicked off an entire, new genre of barleywine. His is extraordinarily hoppy—far spicier and more bitter than the classic English styles, Young's Old Nick or J.W. Lees.

Indeed, the American version as typified by Sierra Nevada Bigfoot Ale or Stone Old Guardian, loudly advertises its manliness, with an ample mouthful of malt and a bitter broadside of hops.

Speaking of his award-winning (10.2% abv) Old Ruffian, Great Divide Brewing founder Brian Dunn said, "We were looking to design a classic American-style barleywine. Something that was significantly more hoppy than the English style, but something that had some balance... I mean, the fact is, when you're going to have a 90 IBU beer, in my mind, you better have a lot of malty sweetness, and not just one dimensional malt, but something with caramel and fruit notes."

Bittersweet complexity, not just brute force, is barleywine's essence. It is for hopheads, not knuckleheads.

Barleywine checklist

- ☐ Alaskan Barleywine
- ☐ Alesmith Old Numbskull
- ☐ Alley Kat Olde Deuteronomy
- ☐ **Anchor Old Foghorn**
- ☐ Avery Hog Heaven
- ☐ Bell's Third Coast Old Ale
- ☐ Boulder Killer Penguin
- ☐ Bridgeport Old Knucklehead
- ☐ Cucapá Barley Wine Ale (Mexico)
- ☐ Dogfish Head Olde School
- ☐ Dominion Millennium
- ☐ Durham Benedictus (England)
- ☐ East End Gratitude
- ☐ Firestone Walker Abacus
- ☐ Fish Tale Leviathan
- ☐ Founders Nemesis
- ☐ Full Sail Old Boardhead
- ☐ Fullers Golden Pride (England)
- ☐ Great Divide Old Ruffian
- ☐ Green Flash Barleywine
- ☐ Hair of the Dog Doggie Claws
- ☐ Hair of the Dog Fred
- ☐ **Lagunitas Olde Gnarleywine**
- ☐ Left Hand Widdershins
- ☐ Mad River John Barleycorn
- ☐ Mendocino Talon
- ☐ Middle Ages Druid Fluid
- ☐ Mikkeller Big Worse (Denmark)
- ☐ Nøgne Ø #100 (Norway)
- ☐ Pike Old Bawdy
- ☐ Nørrebro Little Korkny Ale (Denmark)
- ☐ O'Hanlon's Thomas Hardy's Ale (England)
- ☐ Red Hook Treblehook
- ☐ Rock Art Vermonster
- ☐ Rogue Old Crustacean
- ☐ **Sierra Nevada Bigfoot Ale**
- ☐ Real Ale Sisyphus
- ☐ Smuttynose Barleywine
- ☐ Solstice D'hiver (Canada)
- ☐ Southern Tier Backburner
- ☐ Speakeasy Old Godfather
- ☐ Stone Old Guardian
- ☐ Thomas Hooker Old Marley
- ☐ Three Floyds Behemoth Blonde
- ☐ Troegs Flying Mouflan
- ☐ Twisted Hop Enigma (New Zeland)
- ☐ **Victory Old Horizontal**

Cascadian Dark Ale

Inspiration finds its way into the brew kettle in many a way. Sometimes through the grain bill, sometimes during the boil. And sometimes through the idle conversation of two home brewers happily working on their latest creation, as was the case in 2007 when a Portland, Oregon, beer writer named Abram Goldman-Armstrong and his friend, Bill Wood, brewed a dark ale inspired by Phillips Brewing's Black Toque.

The Canadian-brewed ale was arguably the first of its type to be bottled and widely distributed. It was dark and hoppy like a porter, but you really couldn't call it that because it lacked the style's traditional heavy body. If you closed your eyes, you might think it was a basic IPA. But, of course, this new beer shared none of the British style's grand history and, worse, a "Black India Pale Ale" was a clunky oxymoron.

Here was a brand, new style of beer—a classic example of rule-breaking innovation. And it didn't have a name.

What should they call it? The two brewers joked that they better come up with something before San Diego's brewers (who were then claiming Double IPAs as their own) co-opted the emerging style.

It was Wood who suggested—perhaps in a bit of tongue-in-cheek parochialism—Cascadian Dark Ale.

"Looking back," Goldman-Armstrong said, "it just made a lot of sense."

Fearing that, as a growing number of brewers turned to the style, other ungainly names might catch on, Goldman-Armstrong sprung into action. At first, it was friendly arm-twisting, urging regional brewers he knew through his work as a festival organizer to adopt the new name.

Several quickly adopted the name, and beer fans latched on, partly because other names just sounded ridiculous. Portland beer writer Lisa Morrison noted, for example, that "India Dark Ale" would inevitably be shortened to IDA and just confuse bartenders. "CDA is a great bar call," she said.

In early 2010, Goldman-Armstrong organized a CDA symposium in which brewers and beer writers tasted, discussed and finally built a consensus on the style's characteristics.

For one thing, they agreed, a CDA must be something more than a simple IPA that happens to be black. A brewer can achieve the color without added body simply by cold-steeping dark grains or—as in some dark lagers —with de-husked black malt, neither of which provide adequate roasted character, they said.

And for another, CDA must be brewed with the Northwest's distinctively aromatic hops, including

Cascadian Dark Ale

Aroma: : Citrus, pine, resinous hops and hints of roasted malt.

Flavor: Citrus and spicy hop flavor with light-bodied roasted malt flavor.

Bitterness: 40-90 IBUs.

Strength: 5.5-8.5% abv.

Amarillo, Centennial, Chinook and, yes, Cascades. This wasn't just a matter of local pride. When the resins of Northwestern hops mesh with the roasted malts, said some brewers, they tend to produce an almost minty or rosemary quality—a quality that is missing when the ale is made with British Fuggles or East Kent Goldings.

"It's a very different beer," Goldman-Armstrong said when I asked him if he could taste the difference between an IPA and a CDA with his eyes closed. "If you have any palate at all, you should recognize it's a different beer from standard India pale ale."

Goldman-Armstrong drew up some style guidelines and submitted them to the Beer Judge Certification Program (which hasn't acted on them, yet). The Brewers Association reviewed them, too, and had everyone scratching his head by declaring the category would be called "American-Style India Black Ale." ASIBA? Before anyone could get used to that, the organization renamed it "American-Style Black Ale."

Whatever. As Goldman-Armstrong noted, even if the B.A. hasn't officially adopted the name, the notoriously fussy federal Tax and Trade Bureau has, authorizing its use on bottle labels. That's led several breweries to adopt the name, and even the original from Phillips is now called Sckookum Cascadian Brown Ale.

Chalk one up for inspired home brewers.

Cascadian Dark Ale Checklist

- ☑ **21ˢᵗ Amendment Back in Black**
- ☐ Alaskan Double Black IPA
- ☐ Beer Here Dark Hops
- ☐ Blue Hills Black Hops
- ☐ Blue Point Toxic Sludge
- ☐ Boulder Flashback
- ☐ Brewdog Bashah (Scotland)
- ☐ Captain Lawrence 5 Years Later
- ☐ Cigar City Either
- ☐ Cigar City Or
- ☐ Clown Shoes Hoppy Feet
- ☐ Deschutes Hop in the Dark
- ☐ Element Dark Element
- ☐ Flying Monkeys Netherworld
- ☐ Fish Swordfish
- ☐ Grand Teton Trout Hop
- ☐ Heavy Seas Black Cannon
- ☐ Hopworks Secession
- ☐ Lakefront IBA
- ☐ Laughing Dog Dogzilla
- ☐ Lawson's Finest Liquids BIG HAPI
- ☐ Mad River Serious Madness
- ☐ Magic Hat Demo
- ☐ Marshall El CuCuy
- ☐ New Holland Black Hatter
- ☐ North Peak Furry
- ☐ Odell Mountain Standard Reserve
- ☐ O'Fallon Black Hemp
- ☐ Otter Creek Alpine
- ☐ Peak Hop Noir
- ☑ **Phillips Skookum Cascadian Brown Ale** (Canada)
- ☐ RJ Rockers Black Perle
- ☐ Rock Art Black Moon
- ☐ Rogue Black Brutal
- ☐ Sockeye Double Gnarly Imperial Black IPA
- ☐ Southern Tier Iniquity
- ☐ Stone Sublimely Self-Righteous
- ☐ Terrapin Capt'n Krukles
- ☐ Three Heads Skunk
- ☐ Upland Komodo Dragon Fly
- ☐ Victory Yakima Glory
- ☐ Widmer W'10 Pitch Black IPA

Cream Ale

A harsher critic would sip an American cream ale and sniff that the brewer had dumbed down a perfectly good pale ale. Where are the hops? The body?

And he would have a point, because this often-overlooked style is truly a compromise. Head back to the late 19th century, when a new wave of immigrant brewers perfected the American light lager, and put yourself in the shoes of an old school ale maker. Suddenly, everyone's drinking this confounded, brilliantly clear, crisp Bohemian-style lager, and you're still making dark, ponderous ales and porters.

What are you going to do?

Lighten up, of course. Add corn—it's completely fermentable, doesn't leave behind any proteins and even softens the body. Then you've got to knock down some of those fruity yeast esters, so you condition your ale at a cooler temperature, like a lager.

You could call it a dumbed-down ale. But take another gulp, and you might understand that what you've got is a whole 'nother kind of beer. A hybrid. Go ahead, shrug it off. And while you're at it, X-out another classic light ale style: Kolsch, likewise brewed as the northern German response to those confounded lagers.

Cream ale was designed for simple refreshment in an era when beer was little more than something to drain when you climbed down off your John Deere.

That's what drove Clarence Geminn in 1960 to begin making what many regard as the classic modern version of cream ale, at Genesee Brewing in Rochester, N.Y. "We always considered ourselves a true ale brewery," said his son, Gary, who brewed countless batches himself during a 42-year span at the facility. "My father was looking for something a little milder than our 12 Horse Ale. Something a little less harsh, but with a little tartness."

The result was Genny Cream, a beer that eventually became a million-barrel seller in New York and Pennsylvania alone. Its hint of hops aroma and soft flavor (not to mention its cheap price tag) made it a popular go-to draft for anyone looking for something other than the usual industrial lager.

Geminn, now retired from the brewery, won't reveal the exact recipe. "It's still a closely guarded secret after all these years," he says. But he acknowledges it's essentially a blend of that old 12 Horse and the brewery's lager, Genesee Beer. "That gave it a nice balance."

Today, only a few craft breweries bottle cream ale. But it is a fixture at many brewpubs, for the same reason those ale makers turned to it a century ago. It's the ideal style to offer a Coors drinker.

"It's an introduction beer," says Steve Leason, brewmaster and founder of Selins Grove Brewing in central Pennsylvania. "Plus, it's still an ale, so it ferments pretty quickly, which means it doesn't tie up all my tank space."

Leason started making Captain Selin's Cream Ale because it was the favorite of his wife's grandfather. "Pop-Pop loved his Genny Cream," Leason said. "He died at the Blue-White game [a hugely popular springtime intramural

---

Cream ale

Aroma: Sweet corn-like with little hops.

Flavor: Light hop bitterness, moderate corn with a slightly sweet finish.

Bitterness: 15-20 IBUs.

Strength: 4.2-5.6% abv.

football game at Penn State]. When they carried him out, they dug a 40 of Genny out of his pocket."

No pretensions, just pure refreshment.

Cream Ale Checklist

☐ Anderson Valley Solstice Cerveza Crema

☐ Big Rock Warthog (Canada)

☐ Bowen Island Irish Cream Ale (Canada)

☐ Cameron's Cream Ale

☐ Erie Derailed Black Cherry

☐ Full Circle Cluster Fuggle

☐ Furthermore Fallen Apple

☐ **Genesee Cream Ale**

☐ Granville Island Kitsilano Maple Cream Ale

☐ Haverhill Haver Ale

☐ Henry Weinhard's Blue Boar Ale

☐ Hub City Snowbunny

☐ Furthermore Fallen Apple

☐ Lagunitas Sirius Ale

☐ Lake Louie Coon Rock Cream Ale

☐ Laughing Dog Cream Ale

☐ Little Kings Cream Ale

☐ Mt. Begbie Cream Ale (Canada)

☐ Muskoka Cream Ale (Canada)

☐ New Glarus Spotted Cow

☐ Pelican Kiwanda Cream Ale

☐ Pump House Cadian (Canada)

☐ **Sixpoint Sweet Action**

☐ Sleeman Cream Ale (Canada)

☐ Shaftebury Cream Ale (Canada)

☐ South Shore Northern Lights (Canada)

☐ Sun King Sunlight Cream Ale

☐ Taps Red Cream Ale (Canada)

☐ Terrapin Golden Ale

☐ Thomas Creek Stillwater Vanilla Cream

☐ Thomas Hooker Blonde Ale

☐ Trafalgar Cedar Cream (Canada)

☐ Weston Omalley's Irish Cream

Double/Imperial IPA

I f India pale ale gets its name from its legendary ability to withstand the months-long sea voyage from England to Bombay some 200 years ago, what should we call the new breed of super hoppy American IPAs like Bear Republic Racer X or Stone Ruination?

Four years ago, Garrett Oliver of Brooklyn Brewery stirred up things by declaring that to label them as "imperial" or "double" IPAs was "meaningless."

The birth of India pale ale is one of the great stories in the history of beer, he argued, but it has little to do with those supremely hoppy west coast ales.

"Imperial," he noted, is derived from Russian Imperial Stout—a beer that was originally brewed in England for the Russian imperial family. Americans rejected the monarchy over two centuries ago.

And "Double" is just lame.

"Imperial" or "Double" IPA, he said, "discredits, dilutes and damages our brewing history and heritage."

Instead, he suggested in an interview with *San Diego Union-Tribune* columnist Peter Rowe, the style should be renamed, "San Diego Pale Ale." After all, he reasoned, it was San Diego's brewers—including Stone, Ballast Point, Port and Green Flash—who originated the style.

The column sparked the kind of senseless hoo-hah that's usually reserved for Middle East talks.

Some loved the idea. Others said it was wrongheaded because, dude, everyone knows Vinnie Cilurzo invented the Double IPA in 1994 when he was working at the now-defunct Blind Pig Brewery in Temecula, Calif., and that's, like, an hour from San Diego!

Others wondered what the hell a New Yorker was doing sticking his nose into California beer.

And then the whole debate disappeared.

"It was a nice and generous gesture on Garrett's part," Rowe told me, "There was a sense in the San Diego brewing community of, 'Yeah, let's do this!'

> ## Double/Imperial IPA
>
> **Aroma:** Intense citrus hops.
>
> **Flavor:** Tongue-scraping bitterness with just enough malt backbone to make it drinkable.
>
> **Bitterness:** 60— ∞ IBUs.
>
> **Strength:** 7.5-10% abv.
>
>

"But it's faded away. People are calling it imperial IPA or 2IPA."

Some San Diego brewers were reluctant to adopt the term, Rowe said, because they didn't want to be pigeon-holed with only one type of beer. Can't blame 'em for that—but imagine if the brewers of Cologne or Pilsen had taken the same stance centuries ago with their Kolsch and Pilsner.

Which really gets to Oliver's point: The names of beer styles matter.

"I wasn't opposing the beer… but the lazy, uninspired and inaccurate terminology," Oliver told me. "I thought that American craft brewers, as progenitors of so many new styles, should be just as creative with their naming, rather than naming every strong beer 'double something' and every hoppy beer 'something IPA.'"

Indeed, it's already led to the abominable "Black India Pale Ale," which is just a plainly dumb oxymoron. The way things are going, it won't be long till someone brews a Black Blonde or a Pale Dunkel.

So, what to call this style? I say we're looking at this the wrong way.

IPA got its name because its relatively high levels of hops and alcohol presumably allowed the beer to survive that long sea voyage around the Cape of Good Hope. Yet, many of today's English IPAs—clocking in at a paltry 4 percent alcohol with a dainty hop presence—couldn't survive a voyage around the block.

It's the Brits who need to change, for it's American brewers who are making Real IPA.

Double/Imperial IPA Checklist

- ☐ Alpine Pure Hoppiness
- ☐ Arcadia HopMouth
- ☐ Avery Maharaja
- ☐ Ballast Point Dorado
- ☐ Bear Republic Racer X
- ☐ **Bell's HopSlam**
- ☐ Bend Hop-Head
- ☐ Boulder Mojo Risin'
- ☐ Boulevard Double Wide
- ☐ Breckenridge 471
- ☐ Captain Lawrence Captain's Reserve
- ☐ Dark Horse Double Crooked Tree
- ☐ Deschutes Hop Henge
- ☐ **Dogfish Head 90 Minute IPA**
- ☐ Firestone Walker Double Jack
- ☐ Flying Dog Double Dog
- ☐ Founders Double Trouble
- ☐ Garrison Imperial Pale Ale (Canada)
- ☐ Great Divide Hercules
- ☐ Green Flash Imperial IPA
- ☐ Half Pints Humulus Luicrous (Canada)
- ☐ He'Brew Bittersweet Lenny's R.I.P.A.

- ☐ Heavy Seas The Big DIPA
- ☐ Hoppin' Frog Mean Manalishi
- ☐ Lagunitas Hop Stoopid
- ☐ Lagunitas Maximus
- ☐ Marin White Knuckle
- ☐ Moylan's Hopsickle
- ☐ Ninkasi Tricerahops Double IPA
- ☐ Oskar Blues Gubna
- ☐ Port Brewing Hop 15
- ☐ Rogue I2PA
- ☐ Rogue XS: Imperial India Pale Ale
- ☐ **Russian River Pliny the Elder**
- ☐ Sierra Nevada Hoptimum
- ☐ Smuttynose Big A
- ☐ Southern Tier Unearthly
- ☐ Speakeasy Double Daddy
- ☐ **Stone Ruination**
- ☐ Stoudt's Double IPA
- ☐ Surly Furious
- ☐ Three Floyd's Dreadnaught
- ☐ Three Floyds Dreadnaught
- ☐ Victory Hop Wallop
- ☐ Weyerbacher Double Simcoe

Double Witbier

The difference between megabrewers and microbrewers isn't just the quibbling distinction between capital and art. It is epistemological evidence of God.

The big guys take full-bodied beer and turn it into water. Light beer, low-carb beer, American macro-lagers—these once full-flavored innocents were savagely stripped of body and character, defiled with unnatural ingredients and cast to the earth with the vengeance of the devil. They are an evil, soulless abomination.

Behold small-batch craft brews, sacred vessels of the heavens, nectar of the gods. Can there be any doubt that they are the miracle of Jesus at Cana?

You scoff, it's just beer.

I turn to the Holy Word of the prophets, who counsel us that the sign of purity is white: the clouds above, the innocent lamb in the Garden.

Verily I say unto you: If White is pure, surely it follows that there can be nothing purer than *Double* White.

Consider that this beer style's virginal beginnings, as simple refreshment, crisp, divinely flavored with coriander and orange peels, spicy and fruity. Typically made with unmalted wheat and perhaps oats, it is left unfiltered to produce a hazy, pale color with a billowing white cloud of foam.

White Beer—or Witbier, as the ancients of Leuven called it—died from neglect and avarice in the 1950s, martyred by barbarous Sodomites turning to fizzy, yellow beer. It would take a milkman, the son of a dairy farmer, to roll away the stone. His name: Pierre Celis, the white-clad

Belgian saint whose brewery, De Kluis, means "the cloister," a place of spiritual contemplation.

Even as White Beer's resurrection meant salvation for a world of thirsty, lost believers, the true glory of its return would only be manifested when we got our hands on the style over here, in God Bless America.

Double Witbier

Aroma: Citrus with a touch of spice, light hops.

Flavor: Slightly crisp with a smooth malt flavor, tangy spices and moderate to strong sweetness.

Bitterness: 20-30 IBUs.

Strength: 6-12% abv.

"I only wanted to amp it up a bit," said Phil Markowski, the brewer at Southampton Publick House on Long Island, N.Y., who is credited with bottling the first Double White (and whose name, Da Vinci Code symbologist Robert Langdon might tell you, is almost an exact anagram for *"Hark! O, sip milk"*). Markowski added more wheat, more extra pale barley malt, more flaked oats, more of everything. Suddenly, a delicate, 5% abv quaffer had become a full-bodied 7 percent sipper.

"It just kind of morphed," said Markowski.

Surely what we have here is nothing less than indisputable evidence of Intelligent Design.

Southampton Double White isn't just stronger. It's spicier, fruitier, maltier and more complex. Samuel Adams Imperial White (11% abv) is sweet with notes of cloves and cinnamon. Dogfish Head Red & White (10% abv) is citrusy with a robust depth from the addition of Pinot Noir juice.

I look from this page and see doubters—doubters who protest that Double White is a contradiction of terms, that taking a light, refreshing beer style and turning it into something so strong and intensely flavored is itself an abomination.

This faithless lot will declaim it as "extreme."

Verily I say, these people are heretics, and they will burn in hell.

Amen.

Double Witbier Checklist

□ Bavik White Donkey (Belgium)

□ Boulevard Two Jokers

□ Charleville Tripel Wit

□ DeProef La Grande Blanche (Belgium)

□ Dogfish Head Red & White

□ Grand Teton Tail Waggin' Double White

□ Great Divide Double Wit

□ **Hoegaarden Grand Cru** (Belgium)

□ Jan De Lichte (Belgium)

□ Midnight Sun Anchor

□ Mikkeller Not Just Another Wit (Denmark)

□ Mudshark Full Moon

□ Nøgne Ø Imperial DunkelWit (Norway)

□ River Horse Double Wit

□ Samuel Adams Imperial White

□ **Southampton Double White**

□ The Bruery Bottleworks XII

□ The Bruery Imperial Orchard White

□ Voodoo White Magic Of The Sun

□ White Birch Aloha

India Pale Ale (American)

It was Otto, the boorish American thief in "A Fish Called Wanda," who proclaimed, "I love robbing the English. They're so polite." Can there be any other explanation for the absence, more than 20 years after America's craft brewers swiped the Brits' beloved India pale ale, of a single word of complaint from across the pond?

Here is one of the world's classic beer styles, a historic brewing achievement when it was developed more than two centuries ago, a triumphant affirmation of the expanse and greatness of the English empire. Raise a pint of IPA, and you can just feel the glory of the Union Jack, racing around the Cape Horn with a cargo of wooden casks filled with pale ale made hoppier and with more alcohol to survive the brutal voyage to Bombay.

And it has been hijacked by the colonists.

OK, "swiped" and "hijacked" may be needless pejoratives. In more civilized circles, brewers (and writers) like to say they were "inspired" by their colleagues.

Yet, that hardly describes what the Americans have done with IPA. Compare a glass of Bass Ale, one of the originals, to Dogfish Head 60 Minute IPA. The British version tickles you with a light floral aroma and not much else. The Delaware destroyer wallops you in the face with a grapefruit, like Jimmy Cagney in "The Public Enemy."

An unfair comparison, perhaps, but overall today's American IPA is a thoroughly different ale from its father. It is hoppier, it has more aroma, it has more alcohol, it has more flavor.

You might even say it's better. And even if you won't, Michael Jackson, the British beer critic, sure did. In one memorable column he complained, "Should I desire a true

India pale ale, the style's country of origin, England, would have a hard time delivering; the American examples are far more assertive."

We own the Brits, dude.

Not everybody agrees.

Lately, I've been hearing rumbles that IPAs and other American ales are too… too much. They praise outstanding British IPAs from Meantime, Samuel Smith's and Timothy Taylor and scoff at Americans that hit you over the head with a bale of Chinook and a waft of alcohol. A proper IPA, they cluck, should be softer, rounder and, by all means, it should be cask-conditioned. IPAs should be more like the British: subtle and… polite.

Rubbish.

This ignores one of the signature features of American microbrewing: the celebration of hops. A good IPA in particular, said Brian O'Reilly, the brewer at

American IPA
Aroma: Citrus or floral hops.
Flavor: Assertive hops with a bitter kick. Medium malt sweetness.
Bitterness: 40-70 IBUs.
Strength: 5.5-7.5% abv.

Pennsylvania's Sly Fox Brewery, "lets you understand the role of hops." Indeed, his so-called IPA Project produced a string of single-hop IPAs, allowing patrons to savor the difference between Cascade and Simcoe and even, yes, Target from Great Britain.

"We've totally redefined the India pale ale in America," O'Reilly said. "It's a very extreme beer, the way it's made now."

Extreme, however, is not the same as Otto's boorishness; there's no reason Americans can't be polite, too.

So thanks for the IPA, Great Britain. What else ya got?

American IPA Checklist

- ☐ 21st Amendment IPA
- ☐ AleSmith IPA
- ☐ Anderson Valley Hop Ottin'
- ☐ Avery India Pale Ale
- ☐ **Ballast Point Sculpin**
- ☐ **Bear Republic Racer 5**
- ☐ Bell's Two Hearted Ale
- ☐ Blue Point Hoptical Illusion
- ☐ Boulder Mojo
- ☐ Brasserie Dieu Ciel Corne Du Diable (Canada)
- ☐ BrewDog Punk IPA (Scotland)
- ☐ BridgePort IPA
- ☐ Cigar City Jai Alai
- ☐ Deschutes Inversion
- ☐ Dogfish Head 60 Minute IPA
- ☐ Drake's IPA
- ☐ Elysian The Immortal IPA
- ☐ Firestone Walker Union Jack
- ☐ Flying Dog Snake Dog
- ☐ Full Sail IPA
- ☐ Green Flash West Coast IPA
- ☐ Heavy Seas Loose Cannon
- ☐ Ithaca Flower Power
- ☐ Kocour IPA Samuraj (Czech)
- ☐ Lagunitas IPA
- ☐ Lancaster Hop Hog
- ☐ Left Hand Warrior
- ☐ Lost Coast Indica
- ☐ Magic Hat Hi.P.A.
- ☐ New Holland Mad Hatter
- ☐ Port Wipeout
- ☐ Red Hook Long Hammer
- ☐ Rogue Brutal Bitter
- ☐ Russian River Blind Pig
- ☐ Samuel Adams Latitude 48
- ☐ Sierra Nevada Torpedo
- ☐ Smuttynose IPA
- ☐ Southampton IPA
- ☐ Southern Tier IPA
- ☐ Speakeasy Big Daddy
- ☐ Saranac India Pale Ale
- ☐ Stone IPA
- ☐ Surly Furious
- ☐ Sweetwater IPA
- ☐ **Victory HopDevil**
- ☐ Weyerbacher Hops Infusion
- ☐ Wolaver's India Pale Ale

Malt Liquor

"Minimal taste profile, minimal hopping, lacking in hop bouquet and threshold hop levels…" Fred Eckhardt, *The Essentials of Beer Style*, 1989, describing the style characteristics of malt liquor.

"Get your girl in the mood quicker, get your jimmy thicker, with St. Ides malt liquor." —Ice Cube, *Mix Tape*, 1994, describing the style characteristics of malt liquor.

And there you have it: the grand dichotomy of beer. To some it's all about the flavor, to others it's nothing more than a… um, stiff drink. No other style manifests the distinction better than malt liquor.

Outside of a couple curiosities produced by craft brewers, not a single malt liquor earns a grade over "C" at BeerAdvocate.com. Most earn epithets worthy of terrorist baby killers; there is little praise for any quality beyond its cheap facility for denting one's cerebral cortex. It's got such a bad rep, even those who dependably gripe about "neo-Prohibitionsm" will barely raise a peep in its defense when Bible-thumpers raise hell about the sale of so-called "liquid crack" in inner-city neighborhoods.

Meanwhile, no beer style is so crassly adored as malt liquor.

The Irish might've written odes to their beloved black stout, and Germany treats its lager as religion. But in America, malt liquor—even as it is inevitably packaged in a brown paper bag—is an uniquely identifiable cultural icon.

It is a totem of hip-hop and a punch line on "The Simpsons." An entire generation grew up believing, as Billy Dee Williams told us, that Colt 45 "works every time." You didn't hear the Ramones singing about hefeweizen, though they once shilled for their favorite 40 ("Gimme, gimme, gimme my Steel Reserve.") And the Wayans brothers never made a comedy called "Don't Be a Menace to South Central While Drinking Your Pilsner in the Hood."

Curiously and despite its universal rejection as a serious beer, malt liquor is actually judged every year at the Great American Beer Festival in a category euphemistically called "American-style specialty lager." Yes, the same awards ceremony that has honored the likes of Hennepin Farmhouse Saison has handed out medals to Hurricane, Red Bull, Mickey's and OE 800. (Presumably, the winners received high marks, under the style criteria, for their "sweet-fruity esters and complex alcohols.")

Craft beer, this is not.

The mash is a high-gravity wonder of barley malt, corn grits and dextrose (corn sugar) or fructose (corn syrup). Enzymes are added to fully convert the corn into fermentable sugar, then

Malt Liquor
Aroma: Corn and alcohol, no malt or hops.
Flavor: Dry, corny and boozy.
Bitterness: 12-23 IBUs.
Strength: 6.5—8.5% abv.

a special yeast strain is employed to efficiently boost the alcohol. It is the very definition of a cheap buzz.

Yet, there is a certain fascination with malt liquor among some craft brewers.

Dogfish Head famously packages its Liquor de Malt in a brown paper bag while the Pain Relievaz (brewers Sam

Calagione and Bryan Selders) rap about "pinchin' pennies." Elysian Brewing in Seattle told the Wall Street Journal that its top-selling t-shirt is for AK-47, a malt liquor. And Rogue knows what guys want, packaging potent bottles of Dad's Little Helper Malt Liquor for Father's Day.

There's a fun, healthy sense of irony at work here. But it misses the point because the small brewers' versions of malt liquor actually taste good and, I'm obliged to report, won't make your jimmy any thicker.

Malt Liquor Checklist

□ Camo High Gravity Lager

□ **Colt 45**

□ Dogfish Head Liquor de Malt

□ Earthquake High Gravity Lager

□ Elysian AK-47

□ Haffenreffer Private Stock

□ Hurricane High Gravity Lager

□ King Cobra Premium Malt Liquor

□ Labatt Maximum Ice (Canada)

□ Lightning Ionizer Lager

□ Magnum

□ Mickey's

□ Mohan Old Monk 10000

□ Molson XXX (Canada)

□ Olde English 800

□ Red Horse Malt Liquor (Philippines)

□ Rogue Dad's Little Helper

□ Schlitz Bull Ice

□ Schlitz High Gravity Very Smooth Lager

□ Schlitz Malt Liquor

□ St. Ides High Gravity

□ **Steel Reserve 211**

□ The Bruery Cornballer

□ The People's Pint Tap and Die Malt Liquor

Pre-Prohibition Lager

If we're living in the best of beer times— an unprecedented era of expansive choice, inventive styles and technological superiority— how do you explain the aberration that's come to be called Pre-Pro?

Now, you can count me among the corps of traditionalists who hold it as an article of faith that older is better than new. I prefer worn jeans, experienced women and baseball played on grass.

But there's no way that you'll convince me that beer brewed before the invention of the flip-top can was any better, or even more "authentic," than what we're drinking today.

Nonetheless, nostalgia-minded brewers have jumped in the Wayback Machine to dig up old recipes from those heady days of yore. Session Lager from Full Steam calls itself "a classic all-malt pre-Prohibition style lager." Nebraska's Lucky Bucket says its pre-Prohibition style "salutes a time when lagers had greater character and more distinct flavor, when beer wasn't full of the additives found in many of today's mainstream lagers." Brooklyn Lager describes itself as "a revival of Brooklyn's pre-Prohibition all-malt beers."

All of these are fine beers—pure, smooth, malty, refreshing and satisfying, exactly what you might imagine filled those kegs that Carrie Nation smashed with her axe.

Only, none of them is what our great-grandfathers were actually drinking before the Prohibition. By the time the 18th Amendment rolled around, America was already hooked on corn and rice.

Scroll through the authoritative 1902 *American Handy-Book of the Brewing, Malting and Auxiliary Trades* by Wahl & Henius (go ahead, it's on Google Books), and you'll find that by the early 20th century U.S. brewers had adopted and praised corn and rice as suitable adjuncts to traditional barley malt.

Really, they had little choice.

By then, beer-drinkers around the world were favoring clear, golden and light over murky, brown and heavy. Bohemia had its Pilsener, Germany had its Helles... and America?

Pre-Prohibition Lager

Aroma: Corn or sweet maltiness, with moderately high hops

Flavor: Light malt sweetness with grainy, corn-like sweetness, noticeable hop bitterness, long, clean finish.

Bitterness: 25-40 IBUs.

Strength: 4.5—6% abv.

Well, America's earliest beer barons—Adolphus Busch and Frederick Pabst and Joseph Schlitz—couldn't match the old country. Their malt was produced from domestic six-row barley, a variety that contains more protein than the two-row barley favored in Europe. More protein means unsightly haze and a harsher flavor.

The solution was adjunct ingredients. Corn and rice could smooth out the flavor and reduce the haze without adding body.

Brewers found that the cereals "not only gave a paler color, greater stability and other valuable properties to the beer," the Wahl & Henius guide reports, "but also enabled beers to be produced more cheaply, and its adoption speedily became general."

"All-malt Pre-Pro Lager," it turns out, is a contradiction of terms.

If you really want a true taste of what was flowing in saloons way back when, do yourself a favor and track down a glass of Batch 19 made by—hold onto your mugs—Coors.

According to the brewery, the lager is based on a recipe from a brewer's log dating to just before the Prohibition. The company isn't saying, but I'm guessing from its sweetness there's a good bit of corn.

It's robust, quite smooth, medium-bodied and satisfying.

Which is more than just a little ironic.

For, if Batch 19 is truly authentic, then this fine lager was the first step toward the evil known as Coors Light. After Prohibition, big brewers would continue to lighten their recipes, adding still more cheap adjuncts, softening the bitterness and watering them down till they were utterly lifeless.

Kind of makes you wonder why any craft brewer would want to make a Pre-Pro.

Pre-Prohibition Lager checklist

□ Brooklyn Lager

□ **Coors Batch 19**

□ Craftsman 1903

□ Full Sail Session Lager

□ Genesee Beer

□ Nebraska Lucky Bucket

□ Reading Beer

□ Schell Original

□ Stegmaier Stock Lager

□ Straub

□ Straub Beer

□ Victory Throwback Lager

□ **Yuengling Traditional Lager**

Porter

When it comes to classic British styles, the Americans rule the old world.

Our barleywine is stronger, our India pale ale is hoppier, and our imperial stout is, well, more imperial. Yeah, those are fighting words, and here's some more:

"To say it is equal to any of London, the usual standard for excellence, would undervalue it, because as it regards either wholesome qualities or palatableness, it is much superior…"

That's physician, scientific thinker and author James Mease, writing two centuries ago, on the eve of the War of 1812, about the most American of beer styles, porter. Little has changed over the past two centuries; today's American porter is roastier, hoppier, stronger and—for those who share Mease's patriotism—better.

Indeed, for the early part of its history, American porter was all about patriotism, not to mention the young nation's distaste for all things English.

Porter was a wholly British invention, an aged, slightly sour ale that was brewed dark and strong, earning its name because of its popularity among carriage and train porters.

Its export to the colonies helped define the superiority of our overlords. The professionally trained English brewed with the finest roasted malts; the primitive rabble of the colonies, in contrast, substituted with molasses and licorice. Not surprisingly, colonial boycotts of British goods only occasionally targeted those luscious shipments of porter. You can imagine the patriot Samuel Adams eying wooden casks of fine English ale loaded aboard the ships in Boston Harbor and suggesting, "Hey, let's dump the tea into the harbor instead."

Kicking redcoat butt changed things. Complaining shortly after the Revolution that "we have already been too long subject to British prejudices," George Washington launched a "Buy American" campaign, declaring, "I use no porter or cheese in my family, but such as is made in America; both these articles may now be purchased of an excellent quality."

His favorite: the Philadelphia porter made by Robert Hare, a British-trained brewer who loathed the English.

By most accounts, it wasn't just patriotism that gave American porter its reputation for excellence. There are reports of shipments leaving Philadelphia and making it to Calcutta without spoilage. Meanwhile, writes Mease, repressive English duties on malt and hops forced Britain's brewers to dumb down their famous product with additions of aloe, tobacco, quassia root and sulfates.

Porter

Aroma: Roasty, slightly burnt grains with distinctive hops.

Flavor: Strong malt, but less assertive than stout, with a substantial but not overwhelming hop kick.

Bitterness: 25-50 IBUs.

Strength: 5—7% abv.

By the early 20th century, with Burton pale ale on the rise, porter was all but extinct in the United Kingdom.

In America, the style survived largely because German immigrant brewers—whose crisp, pale lagers would eventually dominate—adapted their early recipes to produce a dark porter made with lager yeast. The hybrid variety is still alive in the form of Yuengling Porter, black, roasty and mildly hopped, but light-bodied, like a lager.

In the early '70s, it was San Francisco's Anchor Brewing who returned us to the early porter that quenched the thirst of our young nation. Brown, smooth and robust, it's a sublime celebration of darkened malts and fresh hops.

Dozens of other American craft brewers followed, and today many of them find that porter is the perfect palette for more adventuresome flavors. Vanilla, coffee, chocolate and smoked malts often find there way into the barrel, with results ranging from curious to astounding.

Back in Philadelphia where it all began, Yards brews porter just blocks from Robert Hare's old brewery. It balances dark malts and molasses with an aggressive but balanced portion of Willamette and East Kent Goldings hops in its nod to the past, George Washington's Tavern Porter.

To say it is equal to any of London... would undervalue it.

Porter Checklist

- ☐ Alaskan Smoked Porter
- ☐ Anchor Porter
- ☐ Atlantic Coal Porter
- ☐ Atwater Vanilla Java
- ☐ Avery New World Porter
- ☐ Ballast Point Black Marlin
- ☐ Bell's Porter
- ☐ Berkshire Drayman's Porter
- ☐ Boulder Planet Porter
- ☐ Boulevard Bully!
- ☐ Breckenridge Vanilla Porter
- ☐ **Deschutes Black Butte Porter**
- ☐ Duck-Rabbit Porter
- ☐ Eel River Organic Porter
- ☐ Elysian Perseus Porter
- ☐ Exmoor Beast (England)
- ☐ Flying Dog Road Dog
- ☐ **Founders Porter**
- ☐ Great Divide Saint Bridget's
- ☐ Fuller's London Porter (England)
- ☐ **Great Lakes Edmund Fitzgerald Porter**
- ☐ Hawkshead Brodie's Prime (England)
- ☐ Highland Oatmeal Porter
- ☐ Kona Black Sand
- ☐ Left Hand Smoke Jumper
- ☐ Mill Street Coffee Porter (Canada)
- ☐ Odell Cutthroat
- ☐ Otter Creek Stovepipe
- ☐ Rogue Mocha Porter
- ☐ Samuel Adams Holiday Porter
- ☐ **Samuel Smith Taddy Porter** (England)
- ☐ Saranac Caramel Porter
- ☐ Sierra Nevada Porter
- ☐ Smuttynose Robust Porter
- ☐ Southern Tier Porter
- ☐ Stone Smoked Porter
- ☐ Summit Great Northern Porter
- ☐ Thirsty Dog Old Leghumper
- ☐ Thomas Hooker Imperial Porter
- ☐ Three Floyds Alpha Klaus
- ☐ Troegs Dead Reckoning
- ☐ Tyranena Dirty Old Man
- ☐ **Yards George Washington's Tavern Porter**
- ☐ Yuengling Porter

Pumpkin Beer

Every autumn they roll out the pumpkin ale, a testament to mankind's genetic impulse to take anything that grows and turn it into booze. Sugar, rice, barley, corn, whatever— let's cook it, ferment it and see what happens.

But pumpkins?

We're talking jack-o'-lanterns, Charlie Brown and Linus, over the river and through the woods to your grandmother's Thanksgiving pie. What kind of sick puppy came up with the idea of defiling an innocent melon with demon alcohol?

Would you believe George Washington?

That's the story from Bill Owens, the former brewer who gets credit for reviving pumpkin ale more than 20 years ago. "I was reading in a brewing book that Washington used squash in his mash," Owens told me a while back. "I thought it was a great idea."

It was 1985, the early days of the American microbrew revolution. Adventurous young brewers, throwing off the shackles of industrial lager monotony, were boldly experimenting with all kinds of ingredients. Owens, who would become an icon in the craft beer movement, was running Buffalo Bill's Brewery in Hayward, Calif.

He tried out a batch of ale with roasted pumpkins, and it tasted, well, like crap. "There was no flavor," Owens said. "If you think about it, pumpkin is basically a neutral starch that converts to sugar. Even if you cook it, there's no real flavor there."

What it was missing, he said, was all the good stuff your mom adds to her pumpkin pie recipe: cinnamon, ginger, cloves. "So I walked to the grocery story across the street, picked up a can of pumpkin pie spices, brought it back and put it in a coffee pot and percolated a gallon of pumpkin pie juice. Voila, real pumpkin flavor!"

Even with a full-bodied taste, it might've been a one-time curiosity, disappearing into history with the likes of vanilla porter. After all, George Washington notwithstanding, America hasn't exactly experienced a long-standing pumpkin ale tradition.

Somehow, though, beer drinkers have gotten hooked on the gourd. For many, it's a nice transition from light summer lagers, putting them in the spirit of the harvest season. For others, it's a twist on October's malty Märzen.

"People just can't wait for the beer every year." said David Buhler, whose Seattle's Elysian Brewing makes no fewer than a dozen different pumpkin styles. Over the years, it's turned out everything from pumpkin weizen to Scottish pumpkin aged in a Jack Daniel's barrel. It even does a secondary fermentation inside a hollowed-out pumpkin, pouring the spiced ale through a firkin tap directly into waiting pints.

Pumpkin Beer

Aroma: Roasted malt with an assertive spice character, very low hops.

Flavor: Maltiness accented with cinnamon, ginger and clove, low bitterness.

Bitterness: varies.

Strength: 4-7% abv.

Yes, Buhler conceded, it's mainly the spices that give pumpkin beer its character. But all that pulp, whether from fresh pumpkins or puree, provides "a depth that spiced beers just don't have on their own... It should remind you of pumpkin pie—not just the taste, but the mouthfeel, the weight, the depth."

Back when Owens brewed his first batch, you might have chalked it up as a passing fad. But no longer. Even Anheuser-Busch brews one.

Pumpkin beer, said Buhler, "just might be the new American Oktoberfest."

Pumpkin Beer Checklist

- ☐ Alley Kat Pumpkin Pie Spiced Ale (Canada)
- ☐ Anheuser-Busch Jack's Pumpkin Spice
- ☐ Bison Organic Pumpkin
- ☐ Blue Point's Mother Pumpkin
- ☐ **Buffalo Bill's Pumpkin**
- ☐ Cape Ann Fisherman's Pumpkin Stout
- ☐ Dogfish Head Punkin'
- ☐ Elysian Night Owl
- ☐ Fegley's Brew Works Devious Imperial Pumpkin
- ☐ Four + Punk'n Ale
- ☐ Harvest Moon Pumpkin
- ☐ Heavy Seas The Great Pumpkin
- ☐ Hoppin' Frog Frog's Hollow Double Pumpkin
- ☐ Jolly Pumpkin La Parcela
- ☐ Michigan Screamin' Pumpkin
- ☐ New Holland Ichabod.
- ☐ Post Road Pumpkin
- ☐ River Horse Hipp-O-Lantern
- ☐ Saranac Bumpkin Ale
- ☐ Sea Dog Pumpkin
- ☐ Shipyard Pumpkinhead
- ☐ Southampton Pumpkin Ale
- ☐ **Southern Tier Pumking**
- ☐ St-Ambroise Citrouille (Canada)
- ☐ Stevens Point Whole Hog Pumpkin
- ☐ **Weyerbacher Imperial Pumpkin**
- ☐ Wolaver's Will Stevens' Pumpkin
- ☐ Williamsberg AleWerks Pumpkin Ale

Rye Beer

R ye is a dirty grain. It is bitter and black and somber-looking. It is unfit for human consumption, except during famine. It is very "disagreeable to the stomach."

This point of view is not mine, for I count myself among those delicatessen faithful who kneel in the presence of pastrami piled high between slices of rye.

Instead, these are the learned words of no less than Gaius Plinius Secundus, a.k.a. Pliny the Elder, the First Century A.D. philosopher who famously scribed a treatise on natural history and then even more famously found his way onto Russian River Brewing's beer labels. When it comes to grain, Pliny wrote, rye takes a backseat to wheat, corn, rice, spelt and almost anything else that grows out of the ground. In the lauter tun, it is a sticky, difficult mess. The few ancient brewers who managed to make use of it—notably in Bavarian Roggenbier and Eastern European Kvass—eventually discovered that those styles would never earn the popularity of beer made from barley.

And yet, Ol' Pliny notwithstanding, rye has found its way back into the brew kettle. The grain has cropped up in at least 500 different brands in just the past decade.

Often, rye is used to give a new twist to a classic style. Founders adds it to bitter pale ale to create Red Rye PA. Great Divide spikes Märzen to come up with Hoss. In its Exit 6 one-off, Flying Fish collaborated with Stewart's Brewing on a Belgian-style ale with a grain bill of 20 percent rye. In all three cases, the rye adds a pleasing, spicy bite to the finish.

Not surprisingly it led to the creation of a singular style known as American Rye Beer.

Brewed as either an ale or a lager, the style is much like American wheat beer, in which the flavor of the grain adds a subtle complexity to barley malt. Often, it is highly kilned, to provide both color and a distinctive—sometimes off-putting—nutty flavor.

It's a delicate balance as brewers find themselves tweaking their recipes from batch to batch. Too much rye, and it's like eating a charred Payday candy bar; too little, and you're left wondering what was the point.

When you get it just right, it comes off something like Summit Brewing's India Style Rye Ale, made with crystal, chocolate and flaked rye. Its spicy tang plays on a nutty, chocolate-like background with just a touch of coffee.

Or Blue Point's Rastafa Rye Ale, a standard IPA that is positively transformed by the addition of rye.

Blue Point brewmaster Mark Burford said that over the years he and partner Pete Cotter have adjusted its rye content between 7 and 20 percent of the total grain. "It took us a while to figure out exactly how to use rye," Burford said. "We're looking for it to add a nutty, spicy complexity to the malt bill."

I often get a bit of tartness in rye beers. Others say they're fruity. Or refreshing, with just a bit of sourness that gets the juices flowing.

Rye beer

Aroma: Rye bread, hold the pastrami.

Flavor: Nutty, with a bit of sweetness and a spicy finish.

Bitterness: 10-50 IBUs.

Strength: 4-7% abv.

But "disagreeable to the stomach?" Look, I realize his name is sacred in certain brewing circles. But in the case of rye, Pliny was wrong.

Rye Beer Checklist

- ☐ 3 Ravens Rye (Australia)
- ☐ Arcadia Sky High Rye
- ☐ Bear Republic Hop Rod Rye
- ☐ Boulevard Rye-on-Rye
- ☐ Blue Point Rastafa Rye Ale
- ☐ Dieu Du Ciel Route Des Epices (Canada)
- ☐ Drei Kronen Schäazer Rogg'n (Germany)
- ☐ **Founders Red Rye PA**
- ☐ French Brod Rye Hopper
- ☐ Goose Island Mild Winter
- ☐ Ithaca Old Habit
- ☐ Lake Placid Honey Rye
- ☐ Madison River Salmon Fly Honey Rye
- ☐ Mayflower Summer Rye
- ☐ O'Hanlon's Organic Rye
- ☐ Paulaner Roggen (Germany)
- ☐ Real Ale Full Moon
- ☐ Samuel Adams Revolutionary Rye Ale
- ☐ Saranac Rye Pilsner
- ☐ Saranac Roggen Bock
- ☐ Schlägl Bio-Roggen (Gerrmany)
- ☐ Schremser Roggen Bier (Austria)
- ☐ Short's Rich's Rye
- ☐ Sixpoint Righteous Ale
- ☐ Störtebeker Roggen-Weizen (Germany)
- ☐ Summit India Style Rye Ale
- ☐ Surly SurlyFest
- ☐ Sweetwater Crank Tank Rye'd Ale
- ☐ **Terrapin Rye Pale Ale**
- ☐ Terrapin Rye Squared
- ☐ The Bruery Acer Quercus
- ☐ The Bruery Rugbrød
- ☐ Tommyknocker Hop Strike
- ☐ Thurn Und Taxis Roggen (Germany)
- ☐ Trafalgar Oak-Aged Rye (Canada)
- ☐ Two Brothers Cane & Ebel
- ☐ Upright Six
- ☐ Wachusett Ryde
- ☐ Wolnzacher Roggenbier (Germany)

Wheat Wine

Barleywine was always a self-righteous beer. For the last 10 or 15 years, it has watched smugly as all the other styles—India pale ale, pilsner, even hefeweizen—were adjusted, adulterated and amped up by American beer makers in their non-stop pursuit of innovation. Barleywine just sat there, arrogant and certain that it was unalterable. With its massive grain bill, heavy-handed hops and potent alcohol content, it was already an extreme beer.

It never saw wheat wine coming.

And who would? Wheat is a woman. She's no threat. Soft, light, she mellows everything she touches.

Watch it! She's a Mata Hari.

Put a glass of wheat wine to your nose and you get that familiar malty barleywine aroma. But hold on. Take a sip and she throttles your throat with silk gloves. Take another and breathe in; you fall into a dizzy swirl of vanilla and apricot and who knows what else.

Wheat seduced barleywine and then took it for all it had. Where was she hiding all this time?

In California, mainly. That's where Phil Moeller of Sacramento's Rubicon Brewing is generally credited with coming up with the wheat wine style in the late '80s. A few other west coast breweries—Marin, Lagunitas, Steelhead—toyed with her over the years.

Wheat wine's myth spread. Smuttynose's David Yarrington got a taste at a craft brewers conference, brought her east and bottled his own version. Foolish man. When he tried to reveal her identity on the label, the feds stepped in. Wheat Wine: Is she a beer or a wine? Or maybe a double agent? Putting her name on a bottle, the feds said, would "confuse and mislead the consumer."

Smuttynose eventually won, and then won again when its Wheat Wine took a gold medal in the Great American Beer Festival's catchall Other Strong Ale and Lager category.

The GABF eventually added a wheat wine category. And that's where she made her final, most seductive move.

Barleywine had always been sure of its manhood. Lots of malt, big alcohol and what beer judges call "assertive bitterness." The assumption among many brewers had been that wheat wine would be the same way. Scott Cramlet, the brewer at Rubicon where the style was invented, said, "It's not really that big of a difference from barleywine. Yeah, there's some wheat character. But in our mind, it shouldn't be all that different. It's basically barleywine that happens to be made with 65 percent wheat."

Wheat Wine

Aroma: Bread-like, caramel.

Flavor: Grainy, bready, fruity.

Bitterness: 50-100 IBUs, and up.

Strength: 8-12% abv.

But the temptress would have her way, as revealed in the fine print in the GABF's guidelines. "Bitterness," it declared, "is moderate to low."

Barleywine never knew what hit it. Wheat wine would be softer, mellower. It wouldn't pull its alcohol punch, but this would be a smoother approach, more like a tight hug.

The gold medal went to Marin's Star Brew-Triple Wheat Ale, a beer that brewer Arne Johnson had recently tweaked by substituting milder East Kent Goldings for more assertive west coast hops. The switch, said Johnson: "Let the wheat come through better."

Famous last words. Wheat was last seen applying lipstick and eyeballing imperial IPA.

Wheat Wine Checklist

□ 75th Street Annona

□ Baird West Coast Wheat Wine (Japan)

□ Big Time Old Sol

□ Boulevard Harvest Dance

□ Bushwakker Centennial Wheat Wine (Canada)

□ Element Vernal

□ Fort Collins Wheat Wine Ale

□ Harpoon Leviathan—Triticus

□ Ithaca Thirteen

□ Jackie O's Wood Ya Honey

□ Lovibonds Gold Reserve Wheat Wine (England)

□ Marin Star Brew Triple Wheat

□ New Holland Pilgrim's Dole

□ Portsmouth Wheat Wine

□ **Rubicon Wheat Wine**

□ Shiga Kogen Wheat Wine (Japan)

□ Ska Wheel Sucker

□ **Smuttynose Wheat Wine**

□ Terrapin Gamma Ray

□ Two Brothers Bare Tree Weiss Wine

□ Weyerbacher Fourteen

Wild Ale

I'm going to make a prediction here, and that is: Anheuser-Busch will never make an American wild ale. The mega-brewery is dabbling with everything else—pumpkin, blueberry, wood-aging, organics.

But the day it willingly infects one of its perfectly made brews with Brettanomyces yeast and packages it as Auggie's Original St. Louis Lambic is the day that cats will sleep with dogs.

It's not so much that the dicey process of rustic fermentation is incompatible with a factory brewery. It's that the taste of wild ale is so far off the charts, so alien to anything its customers would commonly recognize as "beer," that it would never make it to a mass market.

Imagine the focus group tasting, for instance, of Russian River Supplication.

> **Moderator**: OK, here we have a brown ale that was intentionally soured with three different bacterial strains, some of which are common to barnyards and locker rooms. Take a big whiff and tell us your first reaction.
>
> **Participant**: *Ewww....*

The average beer-drinker can't get it past his nose, which only adds to the enjoyment for those of us who cringe at anything that reeks of trendiness. Embrace the funk, breathe in the aroma—American wild ale is the stinky cheese of the beer world. Your reward is layers of unexpected, complex flavors and a redefinition of what beer can offer. The aforementioned Supplication, for example, is flavored with fruit and aged for a year in pinot noir casks, which gives it oak undertones and waves of cherry. Other wild ales taste of spice or pepper or banana.

Always, though, those flavors are accompanied by a mouth-puckering sour wallop.

That sourness—or more precisely, tartness—is the defining trait of American wild ale. Essentially, it's beer gone bad, contaminated by the very stray micro-organisms that Louis Pasteur discovered more than a century ago were mucking up perfectly good beer.

Belgian artisan brewers like Cantillon and Boon still famously allow their beer to be infected, through spontaneous fermentation with ambient bacteria. In America, the new breed of brewers might be daring, but they don't take that risk. Instead, they purposely inoculate batches with controlled doses of Lactobacillus, Pediococcus and that darling of mouth-puckering beer freaks, Brettanomyces, known in brewing circles as just plain Brett.

Wild Ale

Aroma, flavor, bitterness and strength range greatly; no specific standards.

Commercial yeast producers now make bacteria blends so any brewer can mimic the original wild brews of Belgium's Payottenland. No, as the purists predictably whine, it's not a true "lambic."

But so what?

Good, ol' American innovation has led to an astounding variety of wild ale. Russian River blends three different strains of Brett in its Sanctification, New Glarus is re-fermented with Brett found on the fruit skins that flavor its Raspberry Tart, and The Lost Abbey ages its Cuvee de

Tomme (made with barley and raisins) in barrels inoculated with Brett and filled with sour cherries.

Even small brewpubs have found they can work safely with wild yeast with remarkable results. Bethlehem Brew Works in Pennsylvania made a kriek on its 15-barrel system in 2002 that customers are still asking for.

Why, with today's modern brewing techniques, almost anyone can make an American wild ale. Just don't hold your breath waiting for Michelob Framboise.

Wild Ale Checklist

☐ Allagash Confluence

☐ Allagash Interlude

☐ Avery Dépuceleuse

☐ Avery Sui Generis

☐ Captain Lawrence Cuvee De Castleton

☐ Cascade Bourbonic Plague

☐ Cascade Cuvée Du Jongleur

☐ Cascade The Vine

☐ Cascade Sang Rouge

☐ Cascade Vlad the Imp Aler

☐ Cigar City Vuja De

☐ Cisco Cherry Woods

☐ Goose Ialdn Juliet

☐ HaandBryggeriet Wild Thing (Norway)

☐ Ithaca Brute

☐ Ithaca LeBleu

☐ Jolly Pumpkin Bambic

☐ Jolly Pumpkin La Roja

☐ New Belgium La Folie

☐ New Belgium Le Terroir

☐ New Glarus R&D Gueuze

☐ Odell Saboteur

☐ Ommegang Ommegeddon

☐ Russian River Beatification

☐ Russian River Consecration

☐ Russian River Sanctification

☐ **Russian River Supplication**

☐ Russian River Temptation

☐ Samuel Adams American Kriek

☐ The Lost Abbey Cable Car

☐ **The Lost Abbey Cuvee de Tomme**

☐ The Lost Abbey Duck Duck Gooze

☐ Telegraph Reserve Wheat

☐ Weyerbahcer Riserva

Acknowledgements

A reporter is only as good as his sources, and to the many people I've quoted on these pages, I offer a huge "thank you" for taking time to share your wisdom. That especially includes Brian O'Reilly of Sly Fox Brewing, who made the mistake of giving me his cell phone number so I could call him on deadline, Victory Brewing's Bill Covaleski, who taught me to love the Germans, and Garrett Oliver of Brooklyn Brewing, who truly cares about style.

If it weren't for Fritz Maytag, the man who launched the American microbrewing revolution at Anchor Brewing. I doubt there'd be much reason to write about all of these styles. To the friends and family of Michael Jackson, I hope you know that his written words will live forever.

And, finally, to Mrs. Sixpack, Theresa Conroy, who proofread every word and – more importantly – tasted evey beer, it's not enough to say "thank you." A bottle of Westy 12 might do the trick, though.

Don Russell
August, 2011

Joe Sixpack

....is Don Russell, an award-winning Philadelphia newspaper reporter and one of America's best-known beer writers.

He writes a weekly beer column for the Philadelphia Daily News and is the author of two previous books:

Joe Sixpack's Philly Beer Guide: *A Reporter's Notes on the Best Beer-Drinking City in America* (Camino Books).

Christmas Beer: *The Cheeriest, Tastiest, Most Unusual Beers of Christmas* (Rizzoli Universe).

He's also the executive director and co-founder of Philly Beer Week, the world's largest beer celebration of its kind.

Russell lives in Philadelphia with his wife, Theresa Conroy, a certified yoga therapist and studio operator, and their Siberian Husky, Karma.

For more on beer in Philly and beyond, and to order copies of this book, visit JoeSixpack.net.